The Romance of Redemption

By Dr. Chuck Missler

Koinonia House

The Romance of Redemption
© Copyright 2016 Koinonia House Inc.
Published by Koinonia House
P.O. Box D
Coeur d'Alene, ID 83816-0347
www.khouse.org

ISBN: 978-1-57821-684-0

All Rights Reserved.
No portion of this book may be reproduced in any form whatsoever without the written permission of the Publisher.

All Scripture quotations are from the King James Version of the Holy Bible.

PRINTED IN THE UNITED STATES OF AMERICA

Table of Contents

Ch. 1: My Favorite Book 1
   Prophecy as Pattern *2*
   The Heptadic Calendar *4*
   The Law of Gleaning *10*

Ch. 2: Love's Resolve 13
   Names *16*
   In Moab *17*
   A Bond of Love *19*
   The Moabite Stone *22*
   The Seven-Fold Statement *23*
   By God's Grace *25*
   Love's Resolve *27*

Ch. 3: Love's Response 31
   The Kinsman-Redeemer *31*
   The Illusion of Randomness *33*
   In the Field of Boaz *35*
   The Light Turns On *42*

Ch. 4: The Law of Redemption 45
   Zelophehad *46*
   Levirate Marriage *49*

Ch. 5: Love's Request 53
   The Significance of Hems *53*
   The Threshing Floor *56*
   Four Steps *59*
   The Proposal *63*

Ch. 6: Love's Reward 71
   The City Gate *72*
   Boaz at Council *73*
   The Purpose of the Law *76*
   The Kinsman-Redeemer *80*
   David's Genealogy *85*

    The Elder Shall Serve *87*
    Torah Codes in Genesis 38 . . . . *88*

Ch. 7: Selah Moments 91
    The Church versus Israel *92*
    Ruth versus Esther. *93*
    The Title Deed of Planet Earth *94*

Bibliography 103

About the Author 105

Chapter 1
My Favorite Book

The Bible is remarkable in its ability to reach the tenderest parts of our hearts and the roughest corners of our minds. Many of us have a favorite book of the Bible; Genesis, Isaiah, Romans, Revelation – each is powerful and touches us in deep, personal ways. When somebody once asked me to name *my* favorite book of the Bible, I realized the Book of Ruth might easily top the list.

That might seem surprising. Ruth is a small interlude between Judges and 1 Samuel in our English versions, one that tells the simple story of King David's great grandmother. Yet, we find a wonderfully elegant love story in its four short chapters. Ruth holds a great treasure; as a work of literature, Ruth is venerated even in secular college classrooms, but, more importantly, we find the Gospel threaded throughout the entire tale. In fact, it's one of the most dramatic books of *prophecy* in the Bible, and I regard this book as an essential prerequisite to studying the book of Revelation.

In Ruth, we find that every detail carries not just a story of romance, but specifically the Romance of Redemption. It gives us a perspective of God's plan for us, and you and I are profiled here in a very surprising way. In Ruth we discover a concept called the *Goel* – the Kinsman-Redeemer.

We also find here a primer on the distinctions between Israel and the Church. One of the tragic by-products of Christianity today is confusion about God's purposes for Israel. God has a specific plan for Israel and a specific plan for the Church, and in certain ways these are mutually exclusive. They are parallel but separate, and as we read Ruth, we want to remain sensitive to the differences.

The Bible is a masterpiece of communication from a God outside our time domain. The message of salvation is simple enough for the youngest of minds and yet, intellectuals can spend decades studying its pages and still find new hidden treasures in each passage. As we read Ruth, we need to adjust ourselves to multiple levels of understanding.

Prophecy as Pattern

*I have also spoken by the prophets,
and I have multiplied visions, and used
similitudes, by the ministry of the prophets.*

Hosea 12:10

In our culture, we tend to think of prophecy as a prediction with a future fulfillment. That's what we think of as prophecy. That's the Greek mindset, however. The Hebrew model is a little different. Hebrew prophecies about the future are based on patterns. As we study the Hebrew literature, we continually see patterns of the Messiah profiled in Israel.

In Genesis 22, the *Akedah*, Abraham binds Isaac for sacrifice, but a ram is sent to take the place of the young man. It's clear that Abraham knows he's acting out prophecy. In verse 14, Abraham names the place *Jehovah Jireh* – "the LORD will see to it" – or as it was called continually afterward, "In the mount of the LORD it shall be seen." Two thousand years later, on that very spot, another Father did offer His Son. Hebrews tells us that Abraham believed God could raise Isaac from the dead, and in his willingness to trust God and sacrifice Isaac, Abraham acted out the pattern of a prophecy to be fulfilled in the Son of God Himself.

The Book of Ruth certainly has a historical application. The story describes a series of events that actually took place during the times of the Judges. We need to understand the historical period during which these events took place.

There's also a homiletic application in this study. We can take the lessons we learn in Ruth and apply them to our own lives.

We will also discover that Ruth has some prophetic applications. There are mystical revelations that might surprise us if we missed them at first glance. In Hebrew hermeneutics, the rabbis have what they call the *remez* – the hint of something deeper. We run across what appear to be small rabbit holes, but they open the door to another world of perspective.

We find in this story that each of the principal characters represents a character in the greater story of God's love for us. Naomi is Israel, the people of the Pleasant Land, the apple of God's eye. Ruth is the Gentile Believer, the Church, cast out by the Law but brought in by God's grace. Most importantly, Boaz represents Jesus Christ, our Kinsman-Redeemer. He is the husband of the Church, to the blessing of Israel.

These four chapters provide one of the most phenomenal patterns in the Bible. There are critical links in the chain. Like Bethlehem. Why is Bethlehem relevant? Our Christmas cards remind us every year that Bethlehem is associated with the house of David, but why? The throne of David is an important topic. The cross, of course, is the pivotal event in the entire universe. The crown that Jesus is destined to wear also takes a central position in the picture here. We learn about the role of the Kinsman-Redeemer. We also find important clues about the distinction between the Church and Israel, and we want to be sensitive to those issues. Strangely enough, this Old Testament book is the most relevant book for the Church. That sounds like a contradiction, but it's interesting that even the Jewish community always reads Ruth at the time of Shavuot – Pentecost.

The Heptadic Calendar

More than a century ago, Rabbi Samson Raphael Hirsch said, "The Jews' catechism is his calendar." I find his statement very interesting. If we are going to understand the Bible, we need to have a feeling for the Jewish calendar. The feasts of Israel are a yearly reminder of God's purposes and plans, put in place to teach prophetic events in advance.

In the spring, there are three feasts of Israel which represent Christ's First Coming. In the fall, there are three more feasts that represent Christ's Second Coming. In the middle is Shavuot, the Feast of Weeks. The story of Ruth takes place during the barley and wheat harvests, in the early and late spring, centering on the time of Shavuot.

Genesis 1:14 says, *"And God said, Let there be lights in the firmament of the heaven to divide the day from the night; and let them be for signs, and for seasons, and for days, and years."*

The word translated "seasons" here is *HaMoyadim*, which means "the appointed times." The lights in the firmament set signs for highlighting the appointed times. There are 70 specific appointed times in the Jewish calendar. There are 52 weekly Sabbaths each year. Passover Week includes seven feast days. Then there's Shavuot (Pentecost), Yom Teruah (Feast of Trumpets), Yom Kippur (Day of Atonement), and the seven days of Sukkot (Feast of Tabernacles). The end of Sukkot is celebrated by Shemini Atzeret, the eighth-day assembly. When we add these up, we find a total of 70 of these *HaMoyadim*.

$52 + 7 + 1 + 1 + 1 + 7 + 1 = 70$

The Jewish calendar has a heptadic – sevenfold – structure. We recognize that the week has seven days, and the seventh day is the Shabbat.[1] There's also a particular week of weeks, at the end of which the Jews celebrate the feast of Shavuot, or Pentecost.[2] The religious year is a week of months, from the beginning of Passover in Nisan to the end of the Feast of Tabernacles in the seventh month of Tishri.[3] There's a week of years as well, and the Mosaic Law required the Israelites to give the land rest after each seven-year cycle.[4]

After seven weeks of years – 49 years – there was to be a year of Jubilee in the 50th year, and all debts were to be forgiven.[5] All land was to return to its original owners, and all slaves were to go free. It was a time, twice a century, when the people of Israel were given a clean slate. Peter uses the phrase "the time of restitution of all things."[6]

---

1 Leviticus 23:3
2 Leviticus 23:15-16
3 Leviticus 23:5; 23:39-43
4 Leviticus 25:4
5 Leviticus 25:8-13
6 Acts 3:21

| Hebrew Agricultural Calendar and Feasts ||||
Hebrew Month	Gregorian Month	Harvest Crop	Levitical Feasts/ Other Feasts
Nisan	Mar-Apr	Barley	Passover, Unleavened Bread, Firstfruits
Iyar	Apr-May	Barley	Lag B'Omer
Sivan	May-June	Wheat/ Figs	Shavuot
Tammuz	June-July	Wheat/ Grapes	Fast of 17th Tammuz
Av	July-Aug	Grapes	Tisha B'Av
Elul	Aug-Sept	Grapes/ Figs	
Tishri	Sept-Oct	Olives	Yom Teruah, Yom Kippur, Sukkot
Heshvan	Oct-Nov	Olives	
Kislev	Nov-Dec	Olives	Hanukkah
Tevet	Dec-Jan		Conclusion of Hanukkah
Shevat	Jan-Feb		Tu B'Shvat
Adar	Feb-Mar		Purim

We need to be sensitive to the agricultural calendar as we go through Ruth. On the Jewish calendar, the first month of the religious year is Nisan, in about March or April. That's when the majority of the Book of Ruth takes place. Barley acts as a good winter cover crop, and it matures about 60 days after it begins growing again in the spring.

This is the time of latter rains, when the barley harvest and the flax harvest occurs. This is the time of Passover. The Feasts of Unleavened Bread and Firstfruits take place during Passover week. The Feast of Firstfruits is always the Sunday after the first Sabbath following Passover. This is a strange formula, but this feast therefore always falls on a Sunday.

The next month in the Jewish calendar is Iyar, during which the dry season begins. Then we get to Sivan in about May and June. During Sivan, the early figs ripen and land tending occurs. The special holiday in Sivan is Shavuot, 50 days after the Feast of Firstfruits.

What is Shavuot all about? We know it best as Pentecost, the day the Holy Spirit fell on the disciples with tongues of fire in Acts 2, the day the Church started. It's therefore very interesting that it's the only feast of Moses in which leavened bread is used. It's also interesting that the Book of Ruth is always read in Jewish communities at the time of Shavuot. When I've asked Jews *why*, they say that it is associated with the harvest. On the face of it, that makes sense. Ruth met Boaz while gleaning in his fields. However, like the Church, Ruth was a Gentile who came to trust in the God of Israel. Like the Church, she was grafted into the family of Israel by marriage to Boaz, her Kinsman-Redeemer. In light of Christ's role as our own Kinsman-Redeemer, we see there is something far deeper going on here.

The fourth month is Tammuz, which is the wheat harvest. This is when the first ripe grapes appear, in the June-July time period. In July and August there is the month of Av, when the grape harvest takes place. In a culture without refrigeration, there was no way to get grape juice in the spring. It had to be naturally preserved through a process called fermentation. Those who argue that Jesus only drank grape juice and not alcoholic wine are failing to appreciate that by Passover in the spring, the grape juice *had* to have been fermented into wine. There was no other way to preserve it.

Tisha B'Av – the 9th of Av – is memorable as the day in which both temples were destroyed, hundreds of years apart. Throughout history, a long series of bad things have happened to the Jews on the 9th of Av. The fast on the 17th of Tammuz begins the Three Weeks of mourning that lead up to Tisha B'Av. The 17th of Tammuz also commemorates tragedies that took place on that date, beginning with the day Moses broke the tablets of the Law in fury at the worship of the golden calf.[7] The summer has become a time of mourning in Jewish tradition.

Dates and summer figs are harvested in the month of Elul, the August and September time period. Then in September and October, the early rains start and the olive harvest begins. Tishri is the first month in the Genesis calendar, but it became the seventh month of the Exodus religious calendar. With the early rains come the Feast of Trumpets, the Day of Atonement, and Sukkot, the Feast of Tabernacles.

This is a quick overview of the Jewish agricultural calendar. We need to have a grasp of this as we read the Bible, because the people of the Bible were an agricultural people. Little questions

---

[7] Exodus 32:19

like, "Did Jesus drink wine or grape juice at Passover" can be resolved by understanding simple realities about when the grape harvest took place.

Here's something interesting. If we look for the word *HaMoyadim* as an equidistant letter sequence, we find it only occurs once in the Old Testament. Statistically, we'd expect it to show up five times, but it only occurs once, and it does so in the book of Genesis. In fact, it shows up at a skipping interval of 70, centered on Genesis 1:14 when the Sun, Moon, and stars are given for the purposes of our timekeeping. Was that an accident? Of course not. It is another one of the strange things in the Bible that give evidence of God's design.

המועדים The Appointed Times

- As an *Equidistant Letter Sequence*, it appears *only once* in Genesis
  - Statistical expectation: 5 times in the 78,064 letters of Genesis
- It appears only once, at an interval of 70
- It is centered on Genesis 1:14
  - Odds against this by unaided chance have been estimated at greater than *70,000,000 to one!*

The Law of Gleaning

As we begin reading Ruth, it is also important to understand the process of gleaning. The Hebrew Scriptures have a great deal to say about protecting and providing for the widows and orphans. One of the ways in which the ancient Hebrews provided for the less fortunate was in letting them glean the fields. In Leviticus 19:9-10 and Deuteronomy 24, the LORD orders the Israelites to leave remnants in their fields and orchards so that the poor and stranger and widow and orphan can have something to eat. In other words, the workers were not to go back over their fields a second time; they were to let the less fortunate pick the fields clean.

> *When thou cuttest down thine harvest in thy field, and hast forgot a sheaf in the field, thou shalt not go again to fetch it: it shall be for the stranger, for the fatherless, and for the widow: that the LORD thy God may bless thee in all the work of thine hands. When thou beatest thine olive tree, thou shalt not go over the boughs again: it shall be for the stranger, for the fatherless, and for the widow. When thou gatherest the grapes of thy vineyard, thou shalt not glean it afterward: it shall be for the stranger, for the fatherless, and for the widow.*
> Deuteronomy 24:19-21

This was the Law of Gleaning. When the professional reapers had gone through the field, they would be followed by the widows and other destitute individuals who would *glean* the fields. These would gather whatever leftovers they could find to feed themselves. This was the welfare system of the day – God's way of providing for the poor. Note that the poor still had to work for their food. There were no handouts, except by those providing for their own families.

Naomi is an older woman, and her daughter-in-law Ruth loves her dearly. Ruth goes out every day to glean behind the reapers during the barley harvest, and she brings the grain home to Naomi. The people in town know Naomi, but Ruth is a newcomer to them, and by gleaning for Naomi she earns a reputation for herself.

Gleaning was not always a safe job. It was possible that the young women who followed the reapers might be harassed or harmed by them. However, something very unusual happens. The field on which Ruth happens to glean belongs to a wealthy relative of Elimelech named Boaz, and Boaz notices Ruth. He tells his workers to leave her alone, and he charges her to only glean in his field and not go to another. The plot starts to unfold...

These four chapters represent the greatest love story in history, and in their pages we find abounding treasure. In chapter 1 of Ruth, we'll see love's resolve, when Ruth decides to cling to Naomi. In chapter 2, we see love's response, when Ruth gleans for Naomi. Chapter 3 shows us love's request at the strange, widely misunderstood threshing floor scene. Finally, in Chapter 4 we see the big climax: love's reward, in which the land is redeemed for Naomi and a bride is provided to Boaz.

Let's jump in.

Chapter 2
Love's Resolve

Now it came to pass in the days when the judges ruled, that there was a famine in the land. And a certain man of Bethlehemjudah went to sojourn in the country of Moab, he, and his wife, and his two sons. And the name of the man was Elimelech, and the name of his wife Naomi, and the name of his two sons Mahlon and Chilion, Ephrathites of Bethlehemjudah. And they came into the country of Moab, and continued there.

Ruth 1:1-2

This is an introductory sentence, which explains the background for the story about to be told. This was the time of the judges, which was not a spiritually high time in Israel's existence. In fact, the Book of Judges ends by stating its general theme: "*In those days there was no king in Israel: every man did that which was right in his own eyes.*"[1]

There was a period after Moses but before Israel was given a king when Israel was governed by

---

[1] Judges 21:25

a series of judges. It was one of the spiritual valleys in Israeli history. Not a good time. Within that dark period when the judges ruled, however, we find the ultimate love story. It's a love story at the literary level. It's also a love story at the prophetic and personal levels.

After taking over the Promised Land under the leadership of Joshua, Israel spent the next four centuries in a disappointing cycle. The LORD would give them victory, but after a time the Israelites would turn away from Him. He would then allow them to be taken over by their enemies. The Israelites would then repent and return to the LORD, and He would then rescue them through one of the judges. Over and over again we see this cycle of events. Ruth takes place during this colorful but somewhat dark era.

When our story starts, there is a famine in the land. A man named Elimelech moves his wife Naomi and their two sons eastward into Moab where there is food.

There are a number of famines in the Bible.[2] It's not an uncommon problem, and famine may be a response to the spiritual condition of the country at the time. God had warned Israel that famine was one of the judgments that would come upon the land as a result of their failure to keep the Law:

> *...And your strength shall be spent in vain:*

---
[2] Genesis 12:10, 26:1, 41:27ff; Judges 6:2–5; 2 Samuel 21:1; 1 Kings 18:2; 2 Kings 6:25; 25:3 et al

*for your land shall not yield her increase,
neither shall the trees of the land yield
their fruits.*

Leviticus 26:20

*…And thy heaven that is over thy head
shall be brass, and the earth that is under
thee shall be iron. The LORD shall make
the rain of thy land powder and dust: from
heaven shall it come down upon thee, until
thou be destroyed.*

Deuteronomy 28:23-24

We know there was a famine during the time of Gideon in Judges 6. Israel had again turned to doing evil, so God allowed the Midianites to come in and ravish the land. When the Israelites sowed their fields, the Midianites came in and decimated their crops. This invasion went on for seven years, and the resulting famine covered the entire land of Israel.

This matches the situation in Ruth. The famine must have been ongoing for several years in order to compel Elimelech to take his wife and sons and move to Moab. Centuries before, Moab was born as the result of an incestuous night between Lot and his daughter after his daughter got him drunk.[3] The Israelites are therefore related to the Moabites, but there's no great love between these peoples. Moab hired Balaam to curse Israel

---

3 Genesis 19:30-38

during the Israelites' pilgrimage to Canaan in Numbers 22. Under normal circumstance, the Moabites were barred from participating in the national corporate life of Israel.[4] God purposely kept them separate.

Yet, the relationships between some of the individual Israelites and Moabites was good. When David fled the wrath of Saul, he found a friend in the king of Moab.[5] The two countries were neighbors, and they enjoyed years of peace.

> *And Elimelech Naomi's husband died;*
> *and she was left, and her two sons.*
> *And they took them wives of the women*
> *of Moab; the name of the one was Orpah,*
> *and the name of the other Ruth: and they*
> *dwelled there about ten years. And Mahlon*
> *and Chilion died also both of them;*
> *and the woman was left of her two sons*
> *and her husband.*
>
> Ruth 1:3-5

Names

We think of names as mere labels. Names in the Bible have much greater significance than we may initially appreciate; they tend to describe *who* people are, just as much as what they are called. We find that the names in Ruth are meaningful, from the very beginning of the book.

---

[4] Deuteronomy 23:3
[5] 1 Samuel 22

אֱלִימֶלֶךְ	Elimelech: "My God is King."
נָעֳמִי	Naomi: "Pleasant."
מַחְלוֹן	Mahlon: "Sickly."
כִּלְיוֹן	Chilion: "Wasting" or "Pining."
עָרְפָּה	Orpah: "Gazelle."
רוּת	Ruth: "Friendship" or "Desirable."

The name of Naomi's husband was Elimelech – "God is my King" – which is very interesting, since the story takes place during the time of the judges when there was no king in Israel other than God Himself. The names of his two sons are also meaningful. Mahlon and Chilian were apparently given the perfect labels for their short, unhealthy lives. We find in Ruth 4:10 that it was Mahlon who married Ruth.

Naomi's name means "pleasant." When she loses her husband and sons, she suggests they call her Mara, "bitter," instead. Still, her name is "Pleasant," and one of the synonyms for Israel is "Pleasant Land." We can almost see the setup here where Naomi will tend to typify the nation Israel. Orpah means "fawn" or "gazelle." Ruth means "friendship" or "desirable."

In Moab

A full 10 years went by before Naomi heard that the famine had ended. During those 10 years, Naomi's husband died. Her two sons married women of Moab, and then her sons both died. A lot took place during those 10 years, and yet

Naomi did not hear that it was worthwhile to return home until an entire decade passed.

Elimelech came from Bethlehem in Judah, and this is where Naomi intends to return home. There was once a less significant Bethlehem in Zebulun as well. When we talk of Bethlehem, we mean Bethlehem-Ephrathah or Bethlehem in Judah. This is the book that links David to the city of Bethlehem.

In Moses' day, it was the Moabite women who seduced the Jewish men into immorality and idolatry. As a result of that, in Numbers 25 a full 24,000 people died. After that incident, the LORD ordered Moses to smite and vex the Moabites. The Law of Moses did not actually forbid marriage with the Moabites the way it forbade marriage with the Canaanites.[6] But in Deuteronomy 23, the law did forbid the reception of Moabites into the congregation of the Lord until the 10th generation. We're going to see that grace will get around all of that for Ruth, who gives up her people and Moabite god, but that's the general rule.

Now, Naomi finds herself in a desolate position. Her husband and sons are gone, and she has nothing. She's in a foreign country. When they left Judah, they forfeited Elimelech's inheritance. He either sold it or lost it to indebtedness, so Naomi has nothing.

---

[6] Deuteronomy 7:1-3

> *Then she arose with her daughters in law, that she might return from the country of Moab: for she had heard in the country of Moab how that the LORD had visited his people in giving them bread. Wherefore she went forth out of the place where she was, and her two daughters in law with her; and they went on the way to return unto the land of Judah.*
>
> Ruth 1:6-7

Judah is Naomi's home, and she hears that the LORD is once again feeding the people bread in her homeland. It is therefore appropriate that her hometown is Bethlehem – the House of Bread. There is a tale being woven here, and the names are not accidental, even Bethlehem, the House of bread.

A Bond of Love

> *And Naomi said unto her two daughters in law, Go, return each to her mother's house: the LORD deal kindly with you, as ye have dealt with the dead, and with me. The LORD grant you that ye may find rest, each of you in the house of her husband. Then she kissed them; and they lifted up their voice, and wept. And they said unto her, Surely we will return with thee unto thy people. And Naomi said, Turn again, my daughters: why will ye go*

with me? are there yet any more sons in my womb, that they may be your husbands? Turn again, my daughters, go your way; for I am too old to have an husband. If I should say, I have hope, if I should have an husband also to night, and should also bear sons; Would ye tarry for them till they were grown? would ye stay for them from having husbands? nay, my daughters; for it grieveth me much for your sakes that the hand of the LORD is gone out against me.

Ruth 1:8-13

There has obviously grown a bond of love between Naomi and her daughters-in-law. The young ladies do not escape and return to their families as soon as their husbands die. No, they want to accompany her. Naomi means "pleasant," and she must have been a loving person. In fact, Orpah and Ruth are willing to follow her all the way to a strange land that is not their own.

Naomi tries to talk them out of it, and we can almost hear a New York Jewish accent here. Obviously she will have no more sons. Even if she did, no woman would want to bother waiting until those sons grew up, especially when there are Moabite men readily available.

Notice, though, that Naomi attributes her suffering and loss to the LORD. She believes that these things have happened because the LORD's hand is against her. At the least, Naomi recognized that the tragic series of events wasn't pure chance, and she's grieved that her daughters-in-law have to share in the misery of what God is doing to her. She loves them and has a mother's heart for them.

> *And they lifted up their voice, and wept again: and Orpah kissed her mother in law; but Ruth clave unto her.*
>
> Ruth 1:14

In other words, Orpah is sad to leave, but she agrees with Naomi, kisses her goodbye, and returns to her own people. Ruth does just the opposite. Orpah disappears into oblivion; we never hear from her again. Ruth *clung* to Naomi and would not leave her side. That's a big deal.

The Hebrew word translated "clave" is *dabaq*, which means "to stick like glue." The very same clause that induced Orpah to return home is what caused Ruth to stay. The fact that Naomi has lost everything – her husband and sons – meant that she needed someone to take of her, and that motivated Ruth to stay. Her sheer motivation was to take care of Naomi. I don't know how many girls feel that way about their mothers-in-law, but Ruth cared more about ensuring Naomi's welfare than she cared about seeing her own family. Still, Naomi tries to talk her out of it:

> *And she said, Behold, thy sister in law is gone back unto her people, and unto her gods: return thou after thy sister in law.*
>
> Ruth 1:15

Naomi encourages Ruth to return to her own people. The Moabites worshiped a different god than the Israelites did. *Chemosh* was the national god of Moab.[7] His name comes from a root meaning, "to subdue" or "powerful." Chemosh was not simply another name for Yahweh, the Creator. He was a pagan god that accepted human sacrifice. This was the god familiar to Orpah and Ruth – the god they grew up with. It makes sense for Orpah to stay with that culture, because that's what she's used to. It's astonishing that Ruth feels distinctively different.

The Moabite Stone

The famed Mesha or Moabite Stone has confirmed many of the Bible's details about Moab, by the way. In 1868, the Mesha Stone was discovered in Moab by a German missionary. It's a four-foot tall black basalt stone that contains 34 lines in an alphabet similar to ancient paleo-Hebrew, and it has great value in confirming the historicity of the Scriptures. First, it mentions no less than 15 sites listed in the Old Testament, which makes it valuable geographically. It was probably erected about 850 BC by King Mesha of Moab, and it describes the Moabites' conquests against Israel and the House of David. This is especially significant because it gives archaeological evidence that King David indeed had a dynasty. Mesha honors his god Chemosh in

---

[7] Numbers 21:29; Judges 11:24; 1 Kings 11:7

terms that echo the Bible's accounts. To appease Chemosh, the inhabitants of entire cities were apparently slaughtered. It recalls similar practices of the Israelites in their conquest of the wicked Canaanites as described in the Book of Joshua. Some pieces of the stone are now at the Louvre Museum in Paris.

There's a discrepancy between Mesha's account and the Bible's account of the same battle because both sides claim victory. This is not a shock, because most Middle Eastern cultures have a hard time admitting defeat. When I was in Egypt, I was startled to discover that the Egyptians celebrated their "victory" in the 1973 Yom Kippur War. It's ridiculous because they got clobbered, but they celebrated as if they had won. The Egyptian leadership tried to create the impression to the people that the war had been a victory for them. This is one thing that makes the Bible unique, in fact. The Bible authors were willing to admit defeat. Their heroes were not their human leaders or their judges. Their hero has always been God, and so the Bible writers maintained a position of humility about the faults of the people of Israel, including their greatest leaders like Moses and David.

The Seven-Fold Statement

And Ruth said, Intreat me not to leave thee, or to return from following after thee: for whither thou goest, I will go;

and where thou lodgest, I will lodge:
thy people shall be my people, and thy
God my God: Where thou diest, will I die,
and there will I be buried: the LORD do
so to me, and more also, if ought but death
part thee and me.

Ruth 1:16-17

Think about that. Ruth was raised in Moab, an idol-worshiping Gentile country. She is willing to abandon everything. She doesn't invoke the god of her ancestors, saying, "Chemosh do so to me." She declares, "The LORD do so to me." She has already claimed Yahweh as the God she considers the authority in her life.

There is a seven-fold statement in the decision that Ruth makes. She states:

1) Whither thou goest, I will go;
2) Where thou lodgest, I will lodge;
3) Thy people shall be my people;
4) Thy God my God;
5) Where thou diest, will I die;
6) There will I be buried;
7) The Lord do so to me… if ought but death part thee and me.

There is a pattern of seven-fold statements and events throughout the fabric of the entire Bible. It's amazing how many passages we dissect only to find declarations with seven parts. This seven-fold formula is used seven times in the books of Samuel and Kings:

1) By Eli concerning Samuel –
   1 Samuel 3:17
2) By Saul of Jonathan's execution –
   1 Samuel 14:44
3) Of Jonathan's friendship with David –
   1 Samuel 20:13
4) By David concerning Nabal –
   1 Samuel 25:22
5) By David concerning Amasa –
   2 Samuel 19:13
6) By Ben-Hadad concerning Samaria –
   1 Kings 20:10
7) By the king of Israel regarding Elijah –
   2 Kings 6:31

I am fascinated with these things because they offer evidence of design. Even though there are different historians and different books, they have a single author: the Holy Spirit. We do not simply find seven-part statements, but we find seven of them.

By God's Grace

Deuteronomy 23:3 states *"An Ammonite or Moabite shall not enter into the congregation of the LORD; even to their tenth generation shall they not enter into the congregation of the LORD for ever."*

It takes 10 generations for Ruth to get residency, so to speak. The Law said Ruth couldn't enter the congregation of the LORD, but by trusting in God's grace and throwing herself completely on His mercy, she received acceptance.

She forsook her land and family and the gods of her childhood, and she allowed herself to be grafted into the tree of Israel.

The Law may exclude us from God's family, but grace includes us if we put our faith in the Kinsman-Redeemer. That's the lesson that lurks in this entire saga. Consider this: the genealogy of Jesus Christ in Matthew 1 includes four women who have very questionable credentials. Tamar committed incest with her father-in-law.[8] Rahab was a Gentile harlot[9] – who became the mother of Boaz, by the way.[10] Solomon's mother was Bathsheba, whom David stole from Uriah the Hittite.[11] Ruth was an outcast Gentile Moabite woman, and the Moabites were a people judged by God.

The sovereign mercy and grace of God is beyond measure. I am fascinated by the extremes God has gone to for you and me. In the very lineage of Jesus Christ we find four women who should not have been there, yet there they are. What's more, the stories of these women are told. We know who they are, and they are named in the very genealogy of the Savior. Mercy rejoices against judgment.[12] Yet, when all is said and done, God does not get what He wants.

What?

---

[8] Genesis 38.
[9] Joshua 2&6
[10] Matthew 1:5
[11] 2 Samuel 11, Matthew 1:6
[12] James 2:13

Remember, God is longsuffering toward us, not willing that any should perish – and He wants everybody to come to repentance.[13] But do all come to repentance? No. So despite His extreme reach for us on our behalf, God doesn't get what He wants. I find that provocative.

Love's Resolve

> *When she saw that she was stedfastly minded to go with her, then she left speaking unto her.*
>
> Ruth 1:18

Naomi saw that she couldn't change Ruth's mind, so she finally relented. She and Ruth began the journey back to Bethlehem together, a journey of about 75 miles up over the Moabite highlands to the Jordan River. This was not a nice, straight line. The two women would have to ascend to the highlands and then descend about 4500 feet to the Jordan Valley. They would then need to make another ascent of about 3750 feet up to Bethlehem, traversing desert territory through the wilderness of Judah.

> *So they two went until they came to Bethlehem. And it came to pass, when they were come to Bethlehem, that all the city was moved about them, and they said, Is this Naomi?*
>
> Ruth 1:19

---

[13] 2 Peter 3:9

This journey is not described for us. In that one verse, we find our protagonists safely arrived in Bethlehem. We need to appreciate that the two women had to make quite a journey to reach their destination, just the two of them on their own. They do make it safely, and here our story really begins.

> *And she said unto them, Call me not Naomi, call me Mara: for the Almighty hath dealt very bitterly with me. I went out full, and the LORD hath brought me home again empty: why then call ye me Naomi, seeing the LORD hath testified against me, and the Almighty hath afflicted me?*

Ruth 1:20-21

Naomi's grief is still great, and she no longer wants to be called "Pleasant." She asks to be called Mara, "Bitter," to match the bitterness of her life.

Naomi declares that the "Almighty" has afflicted her. The word she uses is *Shaddai*, which means "Most Powerful" from the root *shadad* that means "power" or "strength." It's used 48 times as a name for God in the Old Testament, most of which (31) are in the book of Job. Naomi believes that the God who can do anything has turned His hand against her. She does not understand the full love of God for her, nor how her very grief and loss have made the way for great joy. Her path through life has been changed against her will, but the end result is salvation.

> *So Naomi returned, and Ruth the Moabitess, her daughter in law, with her, which returned out of the country of Moab: and they came to Bethlehem in the beginning of barley harvest.*
>
> Ruth 1:22

This little closing phrase is intended to be a pickup – a positive beat. Barley ripened early in the season, before the wheat, and the reapers generally began to take up the harvest in Abib, or April. Sometimes the harvest began as early as March, and it is the first hint of something joyful.

Up until now, this whole experience has been pretty dark. There was a famine that forced Elimelech and his family to leave their homeland. They sought refuge in a strange country, only to have Elimelech die. The sons get married, but then they die. It's a dismal tale so far, but there's a change coming. They arrived back home in Bethlehem at the beginning of the barley harvest. They don't know it yet, but it's the beginning of the end of their troubles and a time of hope for a happy future.

Chapter 3
Love's Response

Naomi had a kinsman of her husband's, a mighty man of wealth, of the family of Elimelech; and his name was Boaz.

Ruth 2:1

The Kinsman-Redeemer

As we read through Ruth, we want to take a special interest in Boaz's role as the kinsman of Naomi through Elimelech. We too have a Kinsman-Redeemer, a descendant of Adam who has redeemed us by His blood. Our Kinsman is "*holy, harmless, undefiled, separate from sinners, and made higher than the heavens.*"[1] Jesus is the One who is able to redeem us to the uttermost. We will take a special interest in the role and the achievements of Boaz.

The word Boaz means "inherent strength." Boaz is also the name given to one of the two pillars of Solomon's Temple. We'll forgo that study for now, but be sensitive to the fact that there is strength in Boaz. That's what the word *Boaz* should come to mean to each of us. He was a mighty man

---

[1] Hebrews 7:25-26

of war and a mighty man of the law, and he's the hero of this story.

It's interesting that Boaz is related to Elimelech, "My God is King," by blood. This is where the plot starts to be really interesting. Israel is bought back from death by our Kinsman-Redeemer, along with the Gentile Church that has embraced Him. In this story, Boaz is the kinsman through which Naomi will be redeemed and Ruth along with her.

> *And Ruth the Moabitess said unto Naomi,*
> *Let me now go to the field, and glean ears*
> *of corn after him in whose sight I shall*
> *find grace. And she said unto her, Go,*
> *my daughter.*
>
> Ruth 2:2

Ruth has already declared that she will care for Naomi, and she is going out to glean to provide for the two of them. Don't be confused by the King James terminology of Ruth's work as gleaning "ears of corn." The Hebrew word *shibbol* has the idea of outflowing, spreading out or branching out, and is better translated, "heads of grain." It doesn't refer to our American corn from which we make corn flakes and corn bread and ethanol.

Ruth took advantage of the food source available in the nearby fields. She told Naomi her intention of going into the fields, and Naomi gave her blessing to it. There is an additional aspect to this, however.

The Illusion of Randomness

There are two concepts in mathematics that we cannot find in the universe. One is infinity. The other is true randomness. We think we understand these concepts, but we can't find any tangible examples of them. We can never actually reach infinity, and true randomness is elusive; we live in a universe of cause and effect, even when the cause is imperceptible to us.

Jurassic Park familiarized America with a field of mathematics called Chaos Theory. Chaos Theory is based on our inability to find true randomness. It describes the behavior of dynamic systems that are sensitive to small initial differences. These tiny variations result in much broader changes when it's all said and done. In the 1960s, meteorologist Edward Lorenz coined the term "butterfly effect," suggesting that the destruction of a hurricane could be affected by a butterfly's wings flapping weeks before. What we call "randomness" is just an appearance.

According to Chaos Theory, the universe has an underlying order, but the multitude of complex variables makes precise prediction impossible. A tiny change in the variables produces a completely different scenario in the weather or stock market.

Mathematicians speak of pseudo-random numbers. There are numbers that approximate being random, but any procedure to get those numbers means they are not random. It may be surprising, but it's almost impossible to create truly random numbers, and yet scientists sometimes need them. In 1955, the Rand Corporation in Santa Monica published a book called *One Million Random Digits, with 100,000 Normal Deviates*. It's easy to think this book is a joke because it simply contains pages and pages of numbers. It seems meaningless to most lay people, but it became a useful tool to mathematicians seeking random numbers. The RAND Corporation had access to the computers of the Department of Defense, and they went through a rigorous process to ensure there was no symmetry, no patterning, no predictability in their pages and pages of digits.

Ironically, the defining characteristic of a collection of random numbers is the total absence of design. We live in a culture that attributes design to randomness, and we have no clue what true randomness looks like. We teach our children that randomness created every fine-tuned machine in nature, including the brilliance of the human brain. We cannot produce machines as fantastic as those within a single-celled organism, yet organic designs are attributed to nothingness, to absence, to the unsystematic bouncing of atoms. I want you to understand the absurdity.

We are familiar with the Anthropic Principle, the observation that the laws of physics and the characteristics of our place in the universe seem precisely calibrated so that life can exist. In 2004, Guillermo Gonzalez and Jay W. Richards published a book, *The Privileged Planet: How Our Place in the Cosmos was Designed for Discovery*. In this book and its accompanying DVD, Gonzalez and Richards argue that Earth is not only uniquely positioned for life to flourish, but it's also positioned to feed our curiosity about the wide world – so that we can *discover* the universe around us. These combined "coincidences" imply teleology – design with a purpose.

There is no true randomness, and even coincidences are suspect. As Proverbs 16:33 states: "*The lot is cast into the lap; but the whole disposing thereof is of the LORD.*"

All of this is to say that, as the rabbis say, coincidence is not a kosher word. When Ruth stumbled upon the field of Boaz, we trust there was no accident in God's plan. Instead, she landed there by God's divine purpose:

In the Field of Boaz

> *And she went, and came, and gleaned in the field after the reapers: and her hap was to light on a part of the field belonging unto Boaz, who was of the kindred of Elimelech.*
>
> Ruth 2:3

I love the way the Holy Spirit phrases it: "*…her hap was to light on a part of the field…*" The word *hap* means "a chance event." It's where we get the term *happenstance*. Ruth doesn't know whose field she chose. She is a stranger and a newcomer. She doesn't know the families of Bethlehem, nor does she possess a family tree. No. She happens on that field. We often say, "There are no accidents in God's Kingdom." *Coincidence* is when God is working undercover, and we see the plot thicken because Ruth's "*hap*" is to begin gleaning on the field owned by a very powerful man who is a relative of her dead father-in-law.

> *And, behold, Boaz came from Bethlehem, and said unto the reapers, The LORD be with you. And they answered him, The LORD bless thee. Then said Boaz unto his servant that was set over the reapers, Whose damsel is this? And the servant that was set over the reapers answered and said, It is the Moabitish damsel that came back with Naomi out of the country of Moab:*
>
> Ruth 2:4-6

We do not know the name of the servant here in Ruth. However, there's an observation I find fascinating; whenever the Holy Spirit is typified by a person in the Bible, it's always as an unnamed servant. For instance, in Genesis 24, Abraham sends his chief servant to return to the land of Abraham's family and find a wife for Isaac. Abraham chooses this eldest servant who "ruled over all that he had" to undertake this important task.[2] Yet, this servant remains unnamed,

---

[2] Genesis 24:2

despite his position and importance as the manager over all of Abraham's possessions. He brings back Rebekah for Isaac. Nearly 60 years earlier in Genesis 15:2, we learn that Abraham's head servant was Eliezer of Damascus. Interestingly enough, though, Eliezer means "comfort" – and the Holy Spirit is the Comforter.[3]

Jesus explains to us in John 16:13, "*Howbeit when he, the Spirit of truth, is come, he will guide you into all truth: for he shall not speak of himself.*"

It fascinates me to see how literally that's applied. The Holy Spirit always portrays Himself as an unnamed servant, and even when He has a name, it is absent from that particular part of the record. Here, Boaz is introduced to Ruth by an unnamed servant. You may think I'm making something out of nothing, but withhold your judgment until you have the whole story coming out here.

The particular servant who speaks to Boaz is the one set over the reapers. He was to supervise the workers, supply provisions for the reapers, and pay them at the end of the day. When Boaz asks him about the new young woman, the servant knows all about her. Ruth has apparently developed a reputation for herself already. She does demonstrate decorum and wisdom in her dealings, as we see in the next verse:

---
[3] John 14:26; 16:7

*And she said, I pray you, let me glean and
gather after the reapers among the sheaves:
so she came, and hath continued even from
the morning until now, that she tarried
a little in the house.*

Ruth 2:7

She didn't just presume upon the field of Boaz. Before she began gleaning, she first asked permission to do so. Boaz obviously likes what he sees in her. He addresses her directly and not only gives her his blessing to glean in his field, but instructs her not to go anywhere else.

*Then said Boaz unto Ruth, Hearest thou
not, my daughter? Go not to glean in
another field, neither go from hence,
but abide here fast by my maidens:
Let thine eyes be on the field that they do
reap, and go thou after them: have I not
charged the young men that they shall not
touch thee? and when thou art athirst,
go unto the vessels, and drink of that
which the young men have drawn.*

Ruth 2:8-9

In other words, he extends his invitation to continue gleaning in his fields permanently. Ruth is free to work there during the barley harvest through April, and then apparently through the wheat harvest forthcoming in May and June. What's more, she is free to follow immediately after the servant girls where the provisions will be most numerous. Boaz has intervened and given her special privileges, and he's taken the position of her protector. He tells the reapers not to harm her, and also important, to give her water when they take it up from the well. Ruth is not a fool. She recognizes the favor she's been given, especially since she is a stranger to Bethlehem and a Moabite woman to boot.

> *Then she fell on her face, and bowed herself to the ground, and said unto him, Why have I found grace in thine eyes, that thou shouldest take knowledge of me, seeing I am a stranger?*
>
> Ruth 2:10

Grace is the basis for Boaz's kindness here. That's going to be very important as the story continues. We also find out that he's already heard about Ruth. Her reputation has preceded his meeting of her.

> *And Boaz answered and said unto her, It hath fully been shewed me, all that thou hast done unto thy mother in law since the death of thine husband: and how thou hast left thy father and thy mother, and the land of thy nativity, and art come unto a people which thou knewest not heretofore. The LORD recompense thy work, and a full reward be given thee of the LORD*

God of Israel, under whose wings thou art come to trust.

Ruth 2:11-12

Isn't that eloquent? He already admires her, because he has heard that she left her whole world behind in order to take care of Naomi. He also heard that she has given up her native gods and has taken the LORD as her God. This has impressed him deeply.

Then she said, Let me find favour in thy sight, my lord; for that thou hast comforted me, and for that thou hast spoken friendly unto thine handmaid, though I be not like unto one of thine handmaidens. And Boaz said unto her, At mealtime come thou hither, and eat of the bread, and dip thy morsel in the vinegar. And she sat beside the reapers: and he reached her parched corn, and she did eat, and was sufficed, and left.

Ruth 2:13-14

The "vinegar" here is *chometz*, a drink made from sour grapes. The Hebrew word here for "reached" is *tsabat*, which means to "seize with the hand" or to "hand out." The word *tsabat* is only used here and nowhere else in the Hebrew Bible, and in the Hebrew it is singular. This means that Boaz personally served her grain with his own hand.

Love's Response

> *And when she was risen up to glean,*
> *Boaz commanded his young men, saying,*
> *Let her glean even among the sheaves,*
> *and reproach her not: And let fall also*
> *some of the handfuls of purpose for her,*
> *and leave them, that she may glean them,*
> *and rebuke her not.*
>
> Ruth 2:15-16

The method of harvest was this: the worker would grasp a handful of stalks with one hand and then cut through the stalks with the other. Whatever fell off from his hand to the ground was left for the gleaners. Take note, however, that it was unusual for a gleaner to be allowed to pick up grain this early in the harvest. Gleaners were normally permitted access to the fields only after the harvesters had completed all their work. Boaz not only tells his workers to let Ruth follow but to drop sheaves for her to pick up – to generously make her way easy.

Many years ago, I received a letter of encouragement from one of our subscribers. It said, "Chuck, what we like about you is that you leave 'handfuls on purpose.'" They clearly used that phrase from our study of Ruth, and I thought it was charming: "Handfuls on purpose."

> *So she gleaned in the field until even, and*
> *beat out that she had gleaned: and it was*
> *about an ephah of barley. And she took it*
> *up, and went into the city: and her mother*

in law saw what she had gleaned: and she brought forth, and gave to her that she had reserved after she was sufficed.

Ruth 2:17-18

An ephah is approximately nine gallons.[4] That's about thirty pounds of barley, enough to feed them both for five days. Naomi recognizes that this is a large amount of grain for one day of gleaning.

And her mother in law said unto her, Where hast thou gleaned to day? and where wroughtest thou? blessed be he that did take knowledge of thee. And she shewed her mother in law with whom she had wrought, and said, The man's name with whom I wrought to day is Boaz.

Ruth 2:19

The Light Turns On

Ruth might be oblivious to the organization of the community, but Naomi is a good Jewish mother. The favor that Boaz gives Ruth is a ray of sunshine after a very dark period in their lives. Boaz *happens* to be one of their close relatives, and now he is showing Ruth great generosity. This turns on a light, and Naomi immediately

---

[4] In his *Antiquities of the Jews*, 8:2, section 9, Josephus states, "Now the bath is able to contain seventy two sextaries." A sextary was a Roman volume measurement nearly equivalent to an English pint. There are eight pints in a gallon, therefore a bath equaled about nine gallons. Ezekiel 45:11 tells us an ephah is equal to a bath.

realizes the implications of what is happening. This is where the pulse quickens and the plot really gets going.

> *And Naomi said unto her daughter in law, Blessed be he of the LORD, who hath not left off his kindness to the living and to the dead. And Naomi said unto her, The man is near of kin unto us, one of our next kinsmen. And Ruth the Moabitess said, He said unto me also, Thou shalt keep fast by my young men, until they have ended all my harvest.*
>
> Ruth 2:20-21

Naomi recognizes that Boaz is a benefactor, but she also sees the additional possibilities. Boaz is the *go'el* in this story – the kinsman-redeemer. He also typifies the role of the kinsman-redeemer in our own story. As we read this tale, we begin to grasp that the Lord Jesus Christ is our *go'el*, and He regards us with the kindness that Boaz regarded Ruth. This is one of the many attributes that makes Ruth so rich and meaningful.

> *And Naomi said unto Ruth her daughter in law, It is good, my daughter, that thou go out with his maidens, that they meet thee not in any other field.*
>
> Ruth 2:21-23

Naomi's starting to coach her and she's going to prepare her for the scene that comes up in the next chapter. She recognizes the favor that Boaz has given Ruth, and she encourages Ruth to continue under his authority and protection.

> *So she kept fast by the maidens of Boaz to glean unto the end of barley harvest and of wheat harvest; and dwelt with her mother in law.*
>
> Ruth 2:21-23

The harvest came in two stages. First came the barley harvest that began with the Feast of First Fruits in early spring and ended with Shavuot, the Feast of Weeks, in late spring. The second stage is the harvesting of wheat, which began about fifty days later than the barley harvest. It began about the Feast of Weeks and continued until mid-summer. Several months pass, therefore, from the barley harvest to the end of the wheat harvest. During this time, Ruth faithfully goes out each day to glean the fields of Boaz so that she can take the grain home to her mother-in-law.

Yet, more comes of Ruth's time in the fields of Boaz than storing up barley and wheat for the winter.

Chapter 4
The Law of Redemption

Because he is closely related to Elimelech, Boaz is eligible to serve as a kinsman-redeemer for Ruth and Naomi. We will discover in Ruth 3, however, that there is one kinsman still closer than Boaz. We therefore need to look at the Law of Redemption and the Law of Levirate Marriage in order to better understand what is happening.

In Leviticus, God describes the Law of Redemption. Members of the tribes of Israel could not sell away the inheritance of their fathers. Israel belongs to God. The Israelites could lease the land out, but they could not sell the title of the land, so to speak, to non-family members. Even then, the lease only lasted for a designated number of years, or until the Year of Jubilee. In that 50th year, the land would return to the original owners. Of course, the Year of Jubilee took place only twice in a century. It might take 40 years to get back the rights to the lands of one's fathers. However, if there were still years left on the lease, the land could be redeemed by paying for those years, and the ownership would pass into the hands of the near relative who redeemed it.

*The land shall not be sold for ever:
for the land is mine; for ye are strangers
and sojourners with me. And in all the
land of your possession ye shall grant a
redemption for the land. If thy brother be
waxen poor, and hath sold away some of
his possession, and if any of his kin come to
redeem it, then shall he redeem that which
his brother sold. And if the man have none
to redeem it, and himself be able to redeem
it; Then let him count the years of the
sale thereof, and restore the overplus unto
the man to whom he sold it; that he may
return unto his possession. But if he be not
able to restore it to him, then that which is
sold shall remain in the hand of him that
hath bought it until the year of jubile:
and in the jubile it shall go out, and he
shall return unto his possession.*

Leviticus 25:23-28

Zelophehad

During the last several chapters of the Book of Numbers, the Promised Land was divided up among the tribes of Israel according to lot. The land was not supposed to be passed around among the tribes, and the matter of the daughters of Zelophehad made this especially clear.

Zelophehad was a descendant of Gilead, the grandson of Joseph's son Manasseh. Zelophehad only begat daughters, which meant that his descendants would lose their inheritance if the land could only be passed down through sons. In Numbers 27, the daughters of Zelophehad petition Moses on their late father's behalf, and the LORD tells Moses to give these women possession of their father's inheritance. He then lays out the general rule of succession for inheritance, from nearest family members outward, so that the land would always remain as close to the original tribe members as possible. If a man had no sons, then his daughters inherited the land. If he had no daughters, then the man's brothers would inherit the land, and so on.

> *And thou shalt speak unto the children of Israel, saying, If a man die, and have no son, then ye shall cause his inheritance to pass unto his daughter. And if he have no daughter, then ye shall give his inheritance unto his brethren. And if he have no brethren, then ye shall give his inheritance unto his father's brethren. And if his father have no brethren, then ye shall give his inheritance unto his kinsman that is next to him of his family, and he shall possess it: and it shall be unto the children of Israel a statute of judgment, as the LORD commanded Moses.*
>
> Numbers 27:8-11

This was important. The land was to stay within the family. In Numbers 36, the tribe of

Manasseh is concerned that the daughters of Zelophehad will lose their possession to their husband's tribe. It was therefore determined that the daughters were required to marry within their own tribe so that this would not happen:

> *So shall not the inheritance of the children of Israel remove from tribe to tribe: for every one of the children of Israel shall keep himself to the inheritance of the tribe of his fathers.*
>
> Numbers 36:7

In Jeremiah 32:6-12, an event occurs in the life of Jeremiah that puzzles most people.

> *And Jeremiah said, The word of the LORD came unto me, saying, Behold, Hanameel the son of Shallum thine uncle shall come unto thee, saying, Buy thee my field that is in Anathoth: for the right of redemption is thine to buy it. So Hanameel mine uncle's son came to me in the court of the prison according to the word of the LORD, and said unto me, Buy my field, I pray thee, that is in Anathoth, which is in the country of Benjamin: for the right of inheritance is thine, and the redemption is thine; buy it for thyself. Then I knew that this was the word of the LORD.*
>
> Jeremiah 32:6-8

Jeremiah knew the captivity was coming, and yet he is instructed to buy land right before the seventy-year captivity in Babylon is going to start. God tells Jeremiah his cousin will come and ask him to buy property as the nearest kin. Jeremiah therefore sees it as God's will, and when the cousin shows up, Jeremiah pays for the property. This is weird because the prophet will not live to return to Israel after captivity in Babylon. Yet, God tells him to buy the land so that after the captivity, Jeremiah's descendants can return and claim the land.

That's what it sets up – redeeming the land. In ancient Israel, the title deed that named the land owner was a scroll, and on its backside it would hold the details for the redemption procedure. It was sealed, and only the near kinsman can break the seal. We need to understand these things, because in Revelation 5 we find another sealed scroll, a title deed for all of the earth, and only the Lamb is able to open it. We can infer that this title deed also lists the details for redemption.

Levirate Marriage

This is another custom that is strange to us. The word _levere_ is Latin for the husband's brother, and this law dealt with a situation in which a husband passed away with no children. In Deuteronomy 25, the law decreed that a widow could go to her brother-in-law and put a claim on him to take her as his wife, to raise up children for her late husband.

If brethren dwell together, and one of them die, and have no child, the wife of the dead shall not marry without unto a stranger: her husband's brother shall go in unto her, and take her to him to wife, and perform the duty of an husband's brother unto her. And it shall be, that the firstborn which she beareth shall succeed in the name of his brother which is dead, that his name be not put out of Israel. And if the man like not to take his brother's wife, then let his brother's wife go up to the gate unto the elders, and say, My husband's brother refuseth to raise up unto his brother a name in Israel, he will not perform the duty of my husband's brother. Then the elders of his city shall call him, and speak unto him: and if he stand to it, and say, I like not to take her; Then shall his brother's wife come unto him in the presence of the elders, and loose his shoe from off his foot, and spit in his face, and shall answer and say, So shall it be done unto that man that will not build up his brother's house. And his name shall be called in Israel, The house of him that hath his shoe loosed.

Deuteronomy 25:5-10

The Law of Redemption

This was called a levirate marriage. If the husband had no brother, the widow would go to the next nearest kin. Now the man who took the widow had to meet four conditions to be eligible. First, he had to be a near kinsman. Second, he had to be *able* to perform the duty of redeeming the inheritance. Third, he had to be able to take on the other duties required, which included taking the woman to wife and avenging the late husband's death if he was murdered.[1] Finally, the near kinsman had to be *willing*. In other words, it was voluntary. It was considered shameful to refuse, but he did have a choice.

The nearest kinsman had to make his "no" official, however. If he chose not to take the wife, she could ceremonially remove his shoe in the presence of the elders at the city gate. The city gate was equivalent to our county courthouse. In this situation, *taking* his shoe symbolized his shame. In other words, if she requested the man serve as her kinsman-redeemer, her *go'el*, and he refused, she could take his shoe as an act of shaming him for not stepping up to the responsibility. As years went by, the custom grew more relaxed. The man would ceremonially turn over his shoe to the woman to signify that he was giving up his opportunity, and it was done. We learn in Ruth 4:8 that handing over a shoe was the method of confirming a legal transaction regarding an exchange of property.

---

[1] Leviticus 25:25-31; Deuteronomy 19:1-13, 25:5-10;

In the Book of Ruth, three laws of ancient Israel are carefully demonstrated. The Law of Gleaning is lived out in Ruth 2. The Laws of Redemption and Levirate Marriage will come up in Ruth 3 and 4.

Chapter 5

Love's Request

We are used to seeing signs of rank on the sleeves of people in uniform. When we see "mosquito wings" on the upper arm of a young military man, we know that he's a private in the Army, and he's served at least six months but not long enough to be given the rank Private First Class. In the Navy, the gold sleeve stripes of a commissioned officer's dress blue jacket are very important in defining a commander versus a captain versus a rear admiral. In the culture of Jesus' time, rank in the society was embroidered on the hem of men's garments.

The Significance of Hems

In Hebrew, the word for "hem" is *shuwl*. It's the border, fringe, or bottom edge of a skirt or train. In ancient Mesopotamia, "to cut off the hem" was to strip a man of his authority. A husband could divorce his wife by cutting off the hem of her robe. A nobleman would authenticate his name on a clay tablet by pressing his hem on the clay. The embroidery on the hem acted as a signature, because the embroidery represented his family and his authority. The fringes on the Levitical garments are described in depth in several places, identifying the wearers as Levites.[1]

One of the most famous scenes regarding hems is found in 1 Samuel 24, but most people don't appreciate the significance of it. Saul is hunting down David, and he just *happens* to enter the cave where David is hiding. David sneaks up on Saul and cuts off the hem of Saul's robe. Then he grieves afterward, as though he's done something terrible.

> *Then David arose, and cut off the skirt of Saul's robe privily. And it came to pass afterward, that David's heart smote him, because he had cut off Saul's skirt. And he said unto his men, The LORD forbid that I should do this thing unto my master, the LORD'S anointed, to stretch forth mine hand against him, seeing he is the anointed of the LORD.*
>
> 1 Samuel 24:4-6

David's men had urged him to kill Saul while he had the chance, but David refused. Yet, David still feels as though he's done something wrong by cutting off the hem of the LORD's anointed. This is because when David cut that hem, he was symbolically taking Saul's authority from him. It was more than just a chunk of cloth. Shortly after he leaves the cave, he goes out and tells Saul, "See! I cut off the skirt of your robe, but I didn't kill you!"

---

[1] Exodus 28:33, 34; Numbers 15:38, 39; Deuteronomy 22:12

In God's covenant with Israel, God says of Israel "I will spread my skirt over you."[2] This is God's way of expressing His covering, His protection over the House of Israel.

On several occasions, people believed they would be healed if they could just touch the hem of Jesus' robe.[3] This was the goal of the woman with an issue of blood. After 12 years of suffering and having no success with various doctors, she trusted that touching Christ's robe was enough to heal her.[4] The underlying idea is that the authority of Christ is in His hem. As soon as she touched the border of His robe, her hemorrhaging stopped:[5]

> *And a woman having an issue of blood twelve years, which had spent all her living upon physicians, neither could be healed of any, Came behind him, and touched the border of his garment: and immediately her issue of blood stanched.*
>
> Luke 8:43-44

According to tradition, the coat that Jacob gave to his beloved son Joseph was a highly prized seamless robe. According to John 19:23, Jesus' coat was also seamless, *"woven from the top throughout."*[6] That is why the soldiers at the foot of the cross did

---

2 Ezekiel 16:8
3 Matthew 14:36; Mark 6:56
4 As Malachi 4:2 states, "But unto you that fear my name shall the Sun of righteousness arise with healing in his wings."
5 Also found in Mark 5:25-29 and Matthew 9:20-21
6 For a study on 100 ways Joseph was a type of Jesus Christ, see See Chuck Missler's Commentary on Genesis.

not want to divide it but chose instead to cast lots for it. They divvied up the other things, but they gambled for His coat because it was too valuable to tear apart.

It's worth noting that the Temple veil was torn when Jesus died.[7] This was a huge, important event. The entrance to the Holy of Holies was rent wide open. Just as significant, the Levites' period of filling the High Priest's role was over. Jesus had become our High Priest. What's more, His hem was not torn, because He is our High Priest forever.

This is all important to take to heart as we approach the famous threshing floor scene.

The Threshing Floor

> *Then Naomi her mother in law said unto her, My daughter, shall I not seek rest for thee, that it may be well with thee?*
>
> Ruth 3:1

It has now been many months, and Ruth has gone out every working day to glean. Every day Ruth brings back food for the both of them, and it's plentiful because of the generosity of Boaz. However, Naomi sees that this is not the best permanent arrangement for Ruth, a young widow with her whole life before her. She understands that Ruth would be much better off in a marriage where she is cared for. "Shall I not seek a rest for thee?" refers to a מָנוֹחַ, *manoach*, a state or

---
[7] Matthew 27:51; Mark 15:38; Luke 23:45

condition of rest and security. In other words, Naomi wants to provide Ruth a *home*.

There are three main issues facing Naomi here. First, she wants to maintain the name of Elimelech among the tribes of Israel, since both her sons are now dead without having produced children of their own. Second, she needs to take steps to protect her own inheritance, which Elimelech had left in Naomi's trust. Finally, she wants to provide rest and security for her faithful daughter-in-law. A marriage between Ruth and Boaz would solve all three problems. However, to make it work, Naomi would need to renounce her own claim on Boaz as a close relative and hand it down to Ruth, the younger widow. Ruth had been married to Mahlon, so she would be marrying and producing a child to continue Mahlon's name.

Naomi is a good Jewish mother, and she realizes that Ruth has found favor with an important kinsman. There's an opportunity here that she understands, and she's clearly been thinking about it for some time. She begins to coach Ruth, whom she knows is a stranger to the Law and Jewish customs:

> *And now is not Boaz of our kindred, with whose maidens thou wast? Behold, he winnoweth barley to night in the threshingfloor.*

Ruth 3:2

Here we need to understand the ancient Israelite threshing floor. This was not a room inside a barn with a concrete floor. The threshing location was usually chosen as a hill saddleback, where there was a prevailing wind, especially in the afternoon and evening. The workers would beat the grain stalks or have cattle tread on them to separate the heads of grain from the plant material. After the grain had been beaten, grain and stalks and all would be thrown into the air in a process called winnowing. The wind would cause the grain to fall a bit downwind, but the lighter chaff would get blown farther. If it was done correctly, the winnowers ended up with two piles. The nearer pile held the grain and the farther, larger pile held the chaff. The grain was harvested and stored away or sold. The unwanted chaff was burned to keep vermin from gathering.

Second Samuel 24:21-25 tells us that David purchased the threshing floor of Araunah, or Ornan, the Jebusite, which later became the site of the Temple. This location was about 740 meters above sea level, while the Jebusite village that became the city of David was farther south. The Temple was later built in that threshing floor area, but note that it was not the peak of the mountain. (The peak was a little farther north, at a place called Golgotha.)

Threshing was done in the afternoon and early evening. The workers would celebrate in the evening with a harvest celebration; then, the owners would go to sleep near the grain so that it wouldn't get stolen. It was not only a time for work but a time of celebration. Typically, the afternoon was spent threshing the grain, and at night they would enjoy a party.

Here Naomi coaches Ruth about how to handle things:

> *Wash thyself therefore, and anoint thee, and put thy raiment upon thee, and get thee down to the floor: but make not thyself known unto the man, until he shall have done eating and drinking. And it shall be, when he lieth down, that thou shalt mark the place where he shall lie, and thou shalt go in, and uncover his feet, and lay thee down; and he will tell thee what thou shalt do.*
>
> Ruth 3:3-4

Four Steps

Naomi gives Ruth four steps to take. We should appreciate that these same four steps are essential for the sinner seeking Christ.

Step 1: "Wash Thyself."

We recognize that Ruth has been working in the fields, and she is certainly dusty and dirty. It makes sense for her to get cleaned up. If you and I are going to bind ourselves to Christ, we must be clean spiritually. However, we cannot do this by ourselves. Our cleansing comes from God through Jesus Christ Himself. Paul tells Titus:

> *Not by works of righteousness which we have done, but according to his mercy he saved us, by the washing of regeneration, and renewing of the Holy Ghost;*
>
> Titus 3:5

This is why our Lord said what He did to Nicodemus in John 3. Nicodemus might have thought that he was a good, religious man, but he needed to be "born again." He needed to be spiritually washed and *regenerated*. We must first be cleansed of our grime, just as Ruth needed to first wash off the dirt from the fields, but we don't do this by "being good." We do it by the cleansing power of Christ's blood and the work of the Holy Spirit.

Step 2: "Anoint Thyself."

After Ruth had washed, she needed to put on oil to make her skin soft, and perfume, if she had any, to make herself smell good. We also must be anointed, and again, we are anointed by the work of God and not ourselves. As John and Paul tell us:

> *But ye have an unction from the Holy One, and ye know all things.*
>
> 1 John 2:20

> *Now he which stablisheth us with you in Christ, and hath anointed us, is God; Who hath also sealed us, and given the earnest of the Spirit in our hearts.*
>
> 2 Corinthians 1:21-22

That is, the Spirit of God is the only One who anoints us. It is He that can teach us all truth, and each one of us needs the teaching of the Spirit of God. That's the only way in the world we can ever understand the Word of God. The Spirit of God must teach us. He is the One who anoints us and seals us and marks us as the children of God. We should not neglect these facts. Paul says:

But as it is written, Eye hath not seen, nor ear heard, neither have entered into the heart of man, the things which God hath prepared for them that love him. But God hath revealed them unto us by his Spirit: for the Spirit searcheth all things, yea, the deep things of God. For what man knoweth the things of a man, save the spirit of man which is in him? even so the things of God knoweth no man, but the Spirit of God.

1 Corinthians 2:9-11

The Spirit of God is able to teach us and lead us and guide us into all truth. It is vital that we have the Holy Spirit as our teacher. Again, John says:

But the anointing which ye have received of him abideth in you, and ye need not that any man teach you: but as the same anointing teacheth you of all things, and is truth, and is no lie, and even as it hath taught you, ye shall abide in him.

John 2:27

This doesn't mean that we dispense with human learning or human teachers. However, we know that if we "Walk in the Spirit" we shall not "fulfil the lust of the flesh."[8] If we are anointed by the Spirit of God, walking in His truth, we will bear the sweet smelling fruits of the Spirit, which are "love, joy, peace, longsuffering, gentleness, goodness, faith, meekness, temperance: against such there is no law."[9]

You and I today are the beneficiaries of that which has been bequeathed to us by the godly men of the past, men whom the Spirit of God has taught. Ruth's second step was important for her and for all of us. She was to wash and then anoint herself.

Step 3: "Put Thy Raiment Upon Thee."

The Hebrew word for "raiment" here is *simlah*, meaning a "dress" or "mantle." Being poor, Ruth probably did not have a "best dress," but this might mean exchanging her clothes of mourning or her work clothes for her better clothes. It might also refer to the outer garment or cape that she should wear to protect herself from the chill of the night. Such a cape would also allow her to remain anonymous.

Our righteousness in Christ is treated as a robe – a robe of righteousness that is put on all those who believe. Paul speaks of it as a garment that comes down over us, covering us, so that when

---

[8] Galatians 5:16
[9] Galatians 5:22-23

God sees us, He also see Christ's righteousness over us.

> *Even the righteousness of God which is by faith of Jesus Christ unto all and upon all them that believe:*
>
> Romans 3:22

If all this time Ruth had been wearing the clothes of widowhood and mourning, that would explain why Boaz had not moved to court her, for he would not impose himself on her as long as she was still in a time of mourning.

Step 4: "Get Thee Down to the Floor."

That is, stake your claim. This fourth step is seen at the threshing floor, where Ruth goes to seek Boaz and to petition him according to the Laws of Redemption and Levirate Marriage. We can do the same. As the writer of Hebrews tells us, we can go boldly to God to seek what we need:

> *Let us therefore come boldly unto the throne of grace, that we may obtain mercy, and find grace to help in time of need.*
>
> Hebrews 4:16

The Proposal

As we read the threshing floor scene, it is understandable that some might think Ruth is going to proposition Boaz sexually. That's what many people presume is going on here. No, it's worse than that, because she's seeking far more than one night from the man. Ruth is to lie down at the feet of Boaz after uncovering them, taking the servant's position in which the servant lies diagonally at the master's feet. The position was a lowly one, and it represents Ruth as a petitioner. Ruth doesn't argue with Naomi. She trusts her and agrees to Naomi's plan. She goes to the threshing floor and does according to all that her mother-in-law has told her to do.

> *And she went down unto the floor, and did according to all that her mother in law bade her. And when Boaz had eaten and drunk, and his heart was merry, he went to lie down at the end of the heap of corn: and she came softly, and uncovered his feet, and laid her down.*
>
> Ruth 3:6-7

Now, Boaz would lie down by one heap of his grain and his servants would be scattered over other areas of his property guarding the heaps of grain there. This afforded a measure of privacy for both Boaz and Ruth. The heaps of the grain would be piled at the edge of the threshing floor, because the center was reserved for the threshing itself.

> *And it came to pass at midnight, that the man was afraid, and turned himself: and, behold, a woman lay at his feet.*
>
> Ruth 3:8

When it says Boaz "turned" himself, the word is לָפַת – *laphath* – which means to bend, turn, or grasp with a twisting motion. In other words, Boaz turned over to feel or grope around. He might have been groping for his mantle, because he realized that his feet were uncovered. He realizes that a woman is there at his feet:

> *And he said, Who art thou? And she answered, I am Ruth thine handmaid: spread therefore thy skirt over thine handmaid; for thou art a near kinsman.*
> Ruth 3:9

This is the key line. Some people think Ruth is propositioning Boaz sexually, but that's not the point at all. It's quite the contrary – and far more serious, by the way – because she's asking him to marry her. She's asking him to take her to be his wife, to cover her with his authority and protection as the kinsman's part in a levirate marriage. Notice the parts of her petition:

Ruth calls herself his "handmaid" using the word אָמָה – *'amah*. She humbly presents herself as one who is eligible for marriage.

Ruth asks Boaz to "spread therefore thy skirt." She uses the term *kanaph*, and not *shuwl*, but it still has the meaning of the border, the fringe, the bottom edge of the skirt of Boaz's robe. It refers to the fact that a man spreads his garment over his wife as well as himself to keep them both warm. It implies his protection and care.

She tells Boaz, "...for thou art a near kinsman." This is where our pulses should quicken. Here is Boaz, the hero of the book, and here is Ruth, putting this proposal in front of him. By invoking the *go'el*, the kinsman-redeemer custom on her own initiative, she has subordinated her own happiness in order to abide by her family duty of providing Naomi with an heir. That's a subtlety that many people might miss. While Naomi is seeking Ruth's best interest in all of this in helping her get a husband, Ruth is also seeking the best interest of Naomi. She is seeking to honor the name of Elimelech and her late husband Mahlon. When Ruth says, "for thou art a near kinsman," she shows her devotion to Naomi and the family of Elimelech.

It's very interesting that no matter how much Boaz has admired Ruth, he waited for her to make the first move toward a personal relationship.

> *And he said, Blessed be thou of the LORD, my daughter: for thou hast shewed more kindness in the latter end than at the beginning, inasmuch as thou followedst not young men, whether poor or rich.*
>
> Ruth 3:10

Boaz is not a young man. Ruth might have found another, younger man to be her kinsman redeemer, but a younger man would have only benefitted Ruth and not Naomi. Ruth has willingly chosen an older man, apparently putting her own happiness on a lower level than her desire to provide for Naomi and redeem the land for her. Boaz continues:

> *And now, my daughter, fear not; I will do to thee all that thou requirest: for all the city of my people doth know that thou art a virtuous woman.*
>
> Ruth 3:11

Ruth has quite a reputation by now, and I think this statement by Boaz speaks volumes. Boaz recognizes Ruth's good reputation among the people of Bethlehem. She may be a stranger and a Moabitess, but she has placed herself under the LORD as her God, and she is well-known to be a good woman, one who would please him as a wife. Yet, here comes the bombshell:

> *And now it is true that I am thy near kinsman: howbeit there is a kinsman nearer than I.*
>
> Ruth 3:12

Ouch. Boaz is excited and pleased that Ruth has asked this thing of him. He is delighted to take this virtuous woman as his wife, but there's a wee problem; somebody else stands in line before him. There is somebody more closely related than Boaz. Another man has the first right to take on the responsibility and privilege of acting as Ruth and Naomi's kinsman-redeemer. Under the Mosaic Law, the duty fell on the closest male relative unless he waived his right of priority. This also may explain why Boaz did not make his own move earlier. Boaz therefore continues the instruction of Ruth that began with Naomi:

> *Tarry this night, and it shall be in the morning, that if he will perform unto thee the part of a kinsman, well; let him do the kinsman's part: but if he will not do the part of a kinsman to thee, then will I do the part of a kinsman to thee, as the LORD liveth: lie down until the morning.*
>
> Ruth 3:13

The Hebrew word used here for "tarry" is *lun*, which carries no sexual connotations. It means "to lodge" and the word for "hotel" derives from this same verb in modern Hebrew. It is clear that there is no sexual element here. In fact, it's quite the opposite; this interaction is kept on a higher plane.

Boaz tells Ruth that he will take care of everything the next day, and then he puts himself under oath: "…*then will I do the part of a kinsman to thee, as Yahweh liveth*…" When they were in the very crucible of temptation, they both proved themselves righteous by choosing integrity over passion. The plan is spelled out, and Boaz says he will get the ball rolling in the morning. Boaz promises the issue will not be allowed to linger indefinitely; the whole matter will be settled within a day. [10]

---

[10] I am grateful to my good friend, Arnold Fruchtenbaum, for sharing his insights into this passage.

*And she lay at his feet until the morning:
and she rose up before one could know
another. And he said, Let it not be known
that a woman came into the floor. Also he
said, Bring the vail that thou hast upon
thee, and hold it. And when she held it, he
measured six measures of barley, and laid
it on her: and she went into the city.*

Ruth 3:14-15

We see that Boaz is providing for Ruth by giving her food for the day, but we don't quickly understand that there's more to it. The six measures of barley are a Jewish code that Boaz sent to Naomi. Ruth wouldn't understand the code, but Naomi would. Why the six measures of barley? Because it took God six days to create the world, and He rested on the seventh. There were six measures poured out, not seven, and this is Boaz's way of telling Naomi that he's not going to rest until this matter is resolved.

*And when she came to her mother in law,
she said, Who art thou, my daughter? And
she told her all that the man had done to
her. And she said, These six measures of
barley gave he me; for he said to me, Go
not empty unto thy mother in law.*

Ruth 3:16-17

Again, the barley was not for Ruth. The six measures were for Naomi, and Naomi immediately understands the message, as she relates in verse 18.

Verse 17 accomplishes two things: it provides a transition for Ruth's exit from the story; from this point on she plays a passive role. It also puts Boaz and Naomi on center stage; from this point on they are the active players. This is strange, because normally the woman makes the presentation of the Levirate Marriage. Instead, Boaz steps in to take care of the whole thing. Notice carefully what Naomi says next:

Then said she, Sit still, my daughter,
until thou know how the matter will fall:
for the man will not be in rest, until he
have finished the thing this day.

Ruth 3:18

Naomi's prayer from Chapter 1 is about to be answered. Ruth will find a *manoach*, or "rest" in marriage. The famine will no longer be a factor since Boaz's gift assures the woman of plenty to eat. Ruth no longer identifies herself with her lower status, but with her own name. "I am Ruth" in verse nine; she is no longer simply "the Moabitess." The Law of Redemption will be played out in Chapter 4. The fourth chapter of Ruth is the climax to this wonderful, elegant love story.

Chapter 6
Love's Reward

Then went Boaz up to the gate, and sat him down there: and, behold, the kinsman of whom Boaz spake came by; unto whom he said, Ho, such a one! turn aside, sit down here. And he turned aside, and sat down. And he took ten men of the elders of the city, and said, Sit ye down here. And they sat down.

Ruth 4:1-2

It's interesting how the elders of the city respond to Boaz. When Boaz asks the first man to sit down, that is, the nearest kinsman, the man does so without question. It is clear that Boaz is someone who is obeyed. He must have been a high-leverage person in Bethlehem – as Ruth 2:1 has already told us, Boaz was *"a mighty man of wealth."* He's also clearly one that people would follow, and these two verses show us that he's a leader. He collects ten elders of the city, because he is about to transact some legal business.

The City Gate

Remember that the city gate was equivalent to our idea of the courthouse or city hall. The elders of the city would meet there and consider the business of the town. The gate was a protected location, and people entered and left the city through it. People in authority over the city could check the credentials of anybody arriving at their town, and if there was an issue to discuss, the elders came together at the city gate to discuss it.

For instance, Abraham purchased a burial place for Sarah at the city gate.[1] The gate was a place to proclaim news, as when Eli waited at the gate for news regarding the Ark.[2] Absalom won the hearts of his supporters by positioning himself as a judge to settle disputes in their favor at the city gate.[3] Kings would sit at the city gate for legal business, and after David mourned over the death of his son Absalom, he returned to sit at the city gate.[4] David's appearance at the gate meant that mourning was over, and the king had returned to the job of governing.

Judgments were made at the city gate. For instance, it was there the manslayer was judged when he fled to a city of refuge as described in Numbers 35. If the accused could prove that he had accidentally caused another man's death and had not deliberately murdered him, then sanctuary

---

[1] Genesis 23:18-20
[2] 1 Samuel 4:13
[3] 2 Samuel 15:1-6
[4] 2 Samuel 19:8

was given to him in a city of refuge. Other criminal acts were also judged at the city gate, and it was a great tragedy when Jeremiah reports that "*the elders have ceased from the gate.*"[5]

Boaz at Council

Thus, Boaz convened a council. We do not know the name of the first man; the "ho!" that Boaz called out keeps this man's name anonymous. We do know there were ten men total, and we know that it took ten men to make up a *minyan*. That is, a quorum of at least ten men was required by Jewish law to be present before a synagogue service could be conducted. With the nearest kinsman present as well as the necessary ten elders, Boaz begins the business at hand.

> *And he said unto the kinsman, Naomi, that is come again out of the country of Moab, selleth a parcel of land, which was our brother Elimelech's:*

Ruth 4:3

The land needs to be redeemed for Naomi. That's part of the dynamic here. Boaz gets down to business and makes the public case that Naomi is in need of a kinsman-redeemer to step up and redeem the land now that she's back in town. Elimelech clearly lost it when he left to Moab, but now Naomi has returned, and the land needs to be restored. Boaz addresses the nearest kinsman

---

[5] Lamentations 5:14

The Romance of Redemption

in front of the council, asking him to take on the role of the *go'el*.

Remember, however, that there are certain requirements for the go'el. Not only must he be a near kinsman and able to perform the job of kinsman-redeemer, he also must be willing – and willing to assume all the obligations involved. All requirements were critical here.

As we read this, we need to appreciate that every one of these conditions pertains to our own situation. We will encounter our own kinsman-redeemer, and in Revelation 5 we encounter a moment in time when the ultimate title deed is brought out. The one who opens it had to be a kinsman of Adam – He had to be a man. He had to be able to do the job – and assume all the obligations involved. Finally, He had to be willing to perform those obligations. It wasn't enough that He had the right or the abilities, He had to be willing as well.

In this case, Boaz informs the other man of his position and opportunity, and the man agrees to redeem the land:

> *And I thought to advertise thee, saying, Buy it before the inhabitants, and before the elders of my people. If thou wilt redeem it, redeem it: but if thou wilt not redeem it, then tell me, that I may know: for there is none to redeem it beside thee; and I am after thee. And he said, I will redeem it.*
>
> Ruth 4:4

Of course, we are all hoping this anonymous kinsman will not do it. If I were casting the movie of this, I would have someone like Charlton Heston play Boaz and Danny DeVito play the other guy. The fellow agrees to redeem the land, and that's where I believe Boaz's heart dropped to his socks. However, Boaz has another responsibility to throw at the guy, and he hopes this will dissuade him:

Then said Boaz, What day thou buyest the field of the hand of Naomi, thou must buy it also of Ruth the Moabitess, the wife of the dead, to raise up the name of the dead upon his inheritance.

Ruth 4:5

Hey ho! Ruth is part of the deal! Boaz doesn't pull his punches here; he lays it right out there. The men present are all aware of the laws involved here: the Law of Redemption from Leviticus 25:23-28, the Law of Levirate Marriage from Deuteronomy 25:5-10, and even the admonition from Deuteronomy 23:3 that a Moabite could not enter the congregation of the LORD until the 10th generation. Here, Boaz confronts the anonymous kinsman with his own personal situation regarding these laws. The kinsman is willing to redeem the land, but he's not excited about Ruth as part of the package.

And the kinsman said, I cannot redeem it for myself, lest I mar mine own inheritance: redeem thou my right to thyself; for I cannot redeem it.

Ruth 4:6

We don't know all the man's reasons for handing over his right to Boaz. He says that it would, "*mar mine own inheritance.*" Perhaps he did not want to raise up a son for Mahlon. Marrying Ruth and producing a son through her meant that the son would legally be the son of Mahlon and the one to inherit the property. The kinsman would thus end up losing both the property and his investment, and that wasn't acceptable to him. We can only speculate about why he felt this would mess up his own estate planning. Whatever his reasons, he takes a pass, and he is free to do so. He is willing and able to redeem the land, but he is either unwilling or unable to redeem the bride, and so he chooses not to act as the kinsman redeemer.

The Purpose of the Law

Now, who was this nameless kinsman? Good question. He stands in a good position to represent the Law, which is not the path for our redemption. The Law cannot redeem us; it simply provides the path that highlights our need for redemption. The Law was given to reveal man's true condition. Paul calls it "*the ministration of death*" and "the *ministration of condemnation*" in 2 Corinthians 3:6-9. He also says in Romans:

Love's Reward

> *Therefore by the deeds of the law there shall no flesh be justified in his sight: for by the law is the knowledge of sin.*
>
> Romans 3:20

Metaphorically speaking, therefore, the nameless kinsman represents the Law, which was never our Savior. It condemns us rather than saves us, because it highlights our sinful nature.[6] It gives us an understanding of our need for a Savior, so that we will turn to the One who cleanses us and brings us into a right standing before God.

Confusion about salvation leads to an issue called "striving." There are at least three things people say that demonstrates they don't understand their true situation:

> Strike 1: "I'm as good as the next guy,"
> Strike 2: "Well, I'm trying the best I can."
> Strike 3: "I try to live by the Sermon on the Mount and the Ten Commandments."

When I run into this kind of reasoning, I always remember Yoda from Star Wars. "Try not! Do. Or do not. There is no try." Salvation has nothing to do with comparing ourselves to the guy next to us or, God help us, with our own striving toward righteousness. Our salvation comes from the Lord, through the blood of Jesus and the work of the Holy Spirit. He is our righteousness.

This matter needs to sink deep into our hearts. If you have any doubt or confusion

---

[6] Romans 3:10, 23

about the true purpose of the Law, dear reader, I encourage you to plunge into the book of Romans. Paul's letter to the church in Rome is probably the most challenging and intellectual piece of writing on the Planet Earth, and it nails this whole issue.

Shoes

> *Now this was the manner in former time in Israel concerning redeeming and concerning changing, for to confirm all things; a man plucked off his shoe, and gave it to his neighbour: and this was a testimony in Israel. Therefore the kinsman said unto Boaz, Buy it for thee. So he drew off his shoe.*
>
> Ruth 4:7-8

That's an interesting thing. The shoe was a symbol of shame to the unnamed kinsman, but to Boaz it was a marriage license. It's also interesting that the writer of Ruth felt obliged to explain the practice to his readers. Exchanging a shoe was a sign of transferring the right of ownership, and it was a custom that arose originally because it signified taking possession by treading on the soil, as Abraham did in Genesis 13:14-18 and as Joshua was told to do in Joshua 1:1-4. We know from Deuteronomy 25:9 that the one who would refuse his duty as kinsman-redeemer would be subject to having the refused woman take his shoe and spit in his face as a sign of his shame. The shame was in her *taking* the shoe from his foot and spitting on him. Here the man volunteers his shoe to Boaz as a sign of an exchange, without involving the public humiliation of being spat upon. The handing over of the shoe was a custom in a variety of legal transactions that involved the exchange of property, no spit required.

It's remarkable which seemingly small details in the Bible turn out to be important. We've already discussed the hems of robes. It is interesting to study the significance of shoes throughout the Bible as well. For instance, Moses removed his shoes at the burning bush in Exodus 3:5. When Joshua was confronted by none other than the Lord Jesus Christ before the battle of Jericho, he was commanded to: *"Loose thy shoe from off thy foot; for the place whereon thou standest is holy."* [7] In Deuteronomy 29:5, we learn that the shoes of the people did not wear out during the entire forty years in the wilderness. In the New Testament, John the Baptist speaks of the Lord Jesus as one whose shoe latches he's unworthy to unloose.[8]

As we study the Bible, we find that the Holy Spirit tends to use the same idioms in the same ways throughout the 66 books of the Bible. This is called the "principle of expositional constancy." The consistent use of idioms is an evidence of a single authorship. We discover that every detail in the Bible is deliberately placed there,

---

7 Joshua 5:15
8 Matthew 3:11; Mark 1:7; Luke 3:16; John 1:27

and that causes us to pay attention to seemingly insignificant subjects like hems and shoes.

The Kinsman-Redeemer

At this point, we near the high point of the entire Book of Ruth. The anonymous kinsman was willing to purchase the land but has declined to take Ruth as his bride. He has yielded his shoe to defer the obligation. Boaz no longer has any technicalities blocking his way.

> *And Boaz said unto the elders, and unto all the people, Ye are witnesses this day, that I have bought all that was Elimelech's, and all that was Chilion's and Mahlon's, of the hand of Naomi. Moreover Ruth the Moabitess, the wife of Mahlon, have I purchased to be my wife, to raise up the name of the dead upon his inheritance, that the name of the dead be not cut off from among his brethren, and from the gate of his place: ye are witnesses this day.*
> Ruth 4:9-10

Boaz steps up and declares before his witnesses that he is purchasing all that once belonged to Naomi's men. Don't miss the fact, however, that this includes Ruth herself. He is buying the land, but he is also buying Ruth as a bride. She's described as being purchased. We don't like the idea of women being purchased, but remember that we too were purchased. It cost Christ His very life to purchase us as His Bride. I personally believe that we will spend an eternity discovering what it cost Him for us to be with Him there.

> *And all the people that were in the gate,*
> *and the elders, said, We are witnesses.*
> *The LORD make the woman that is come*
> *into thine house like Rachel and like Leah,*
> *which two did build the house of Israel:*
> *and do thou worthily in Ephratah, and be*
> *famous in Bethlehem:*
>
> Ruth 4:11

These enigmatic verses sound like a toast at a wedding. The people are giving their approval of the union of Boaz and Ruth, blessing them with a blessing of many children like the mothers of the Israelite nation.

This whole thing is what makes Bethlehem significant. In three more generations, we will find Samuel the prophet entering Bethlehem, sent by God to anoint the king who would succeed Saul.[9] Samuel is sent to call Jesse, a grandson of Boaz, to sacrifice to the LORD with his sons, so that God can show Samuel the man He's chosen as king. Yet, nobody thinks to call Jesse's youngest son, David, who is out in the fields guarding the sheep.

David is the great-grandson of Boaz and Ruth, and Bethlehem is his historical family home. What's more, Bethlehem is the family home of the Son of David, the Messiah. The little town has

---

[9] 1 Samuel 16

become an idiom in all our languages because of the Son born there 1000 years later, placed in a manger among the animals because there was no room for his mother at the inn. Here in Ruth, the people declare that Boaz is famous in Bethlehem, but Bethlehem itself is famous to us because of Jesus' birth. When we read about the shepherds in the field in Luke 2:8-9, I believe those fields originally belonged to Boaz and Ruth. This closes the loop, if you will.

> *But thou, Bethlehem Ephratah, though thou be little among the thousands of Judah, yet out of thee shall he come forth unto me that is to be ruler in Israel; whose goings forth have been from of old, from everlasting.*
>
> Micah 5:2

The wedding toast continues:

> *And let thy house be like the house of Pharez, whom Tamar bare unto Judah, of the seed which the LORD shall give thee of this young woman.*
>
> Ruth 4:12

In our world today, this part of the blessing might sound more like a curse, considering the sordid manner in which Tamar and Judah conceived Pharez and his twin brother Zarah. Tamar produced them with her father-in-law after a failed levirate marriage with Judah's second son. We might think, "That's no way to talk at a wedding," because we do not understand the significance of Pharez. Judah's two oldest sons had died, and Pharez became the first of his sons to have children. The offspring of Pharez became mighty men in the tribe of Judah. 1 Chronicles 2:10 tells us that his descendant Nahshon, was "*prince of the children of Judah*," and Nahshon was the grandfather of Boaz.

The descendants of Pharez became a very great people in the largest tribe in Israel. Ruth 4:12 is a prophecy – a profound prophecy for the house of Boaz. It blesses him with a multitude of descendants and greatness, but there is more to it than that.

Tamar was a widow. Her father-in-law Judah had not given her to his third son, Shelah, as promised, because God had killed Judah's first two sons and he was afraid of losing the third. When Judah's wife died, he sought companionship in a roadside harlot, who ended up being Tamar in disguise. Their liaison was a one-time affair. After discovering that he had fathered Tamar's children, Judah repented and he never touched Tamar again. Still, Pharez and Zarah were illegitimate sons, and according to the Law, a bastard could not enter into the congregation of the LORD until the 10th generation. So, there is a prophecy here in Ruth regarding Pharez, which we shall see shortly.

*So Boaz took Ruth, and she was his wife:
and when he went in unto her, the LORD
gave her conception, and she bare a son.*

Ruth 4:13

It is important to carefully notice that there is a progression of Ruth's station in relation to Boaz. Initially she calls herself a *nokri*, a foreigner, in Ruth 2:10. A few verses later in 2:13, she is referred to as a *shiphchah*, a lower servant. At the threshing floor in verse 3:9, she's an *almah*, a maidservant eligible for marriage. Finally, she is his *ishshah*, his wife. She makes a progression from foreigner, to lower servant, to eligible maidservant, to wife.

*And the women said unto Naomi, Blessed
be the LORD, which hath not left thee
this day without a kinsman, that his name
may be famous in Israel. And he shall
be unto thee a restorer of thy life, and a
nourisher of thine old age: for thy daughter
in law, which loveth thee, which is better
to thee than seven sons, hath born him.*

Ruth 4:14-15

For Naomi, this is as good as it gets. Her land has been redeemed. Ruth has a husband, and she has a grandchild. The other women recognize the great blessings that have been given Naomi, and they rejoice with her over the kindness that God has shown toward her.

*And Naomi took the child, and laid it in
her bosom, and became nurse unto it.
And the women her neighbours gave it
a name, saying, There is a son born to
Naomi; and they called his name Obed:
he is the father of Jesse, the father
of David.*

Ruth 4:16-17

The term "nurse" implies a guardian or nanny in the technical sense. It does not imply a wet nurse. The neighbor women name the child "Obed," which means, "one who serves."

David's Genealogy

We then find an appendage to the story that gives the connection between Ruth and David. First we find that Obed became the father of Jesse, the father of David, then we find a tidy genealogy that leads from Judah's son Pharez down to David.

*Now these are the generations of Pharez:
Pharez begat Hezron, And Hezron begat
Ram, and Ram begat Amminadab,
And Amminadab begat Nahshon,
and Nahshon begat Salmon, And Salmon
begat Boaz, and Boaz begat Obed,
And Obed begat Jesse, and Jesse
begat David.*

Ruth 4:18-22

According to Genesis 46:12, Pharez moved to Egypt with his father Judah and his sons Hezron and Hamul. Hezron was therefore the first generation to grow up in Egypt. Ram is mentioned as his son in 1 Chronicles 2:9. Ram begat Amminadab, and Amminadab begat Nahshon. Amminadab also had a daughter named Elisheba, Nahshon's sister, who married Moses' brother Aaron.[10] This made Elisheba highly important in the history of the sons of Aaron, who were responsible for the Tabernacle and later the Temple. Again, Nahshon was the prince of the tribe of Judah, and he was among those who left Egypt under Moses. His son Salmon entered the Promised Land under Joshua 40 years later, and he clearly settled in Bethlehem. Not only did Salmon participate in the conquest of Canaan, but he may have been one of the two spies who entered Jericho in Joshua 2. Either way, he begat Boaz by Rahab the harlot who hid those two spies. Many years later, as an old man who admired a virtuous young widow from Moab, Boaz begat Obed, Obed begat Jesse, and Jesse begat David.

Back to the prophecy concerning Pharez. Pharez was illegitimate, and bastards were not permitted to enter the congregation of the LORD for 10 generations. This is important, so let's count the generations involved here:

1) Pharez Perez
2) Hezron

---

[10] Exodus 6:23

3) Ram
4) Amminadab
5) Nahshon
6) Salmon
7) Boaz
8) Obed
9) Jesse
10) David

It is in David's heart to build the Temple, but God forces him to hand over that responsibility to Solomon, who is the 11th generation from Pharez.

The Elder Shall Serve

There is a constant theme throughout the Bible in which the older brother ends up serving the younger. We see it in Jacob and Esau in Genesis 25:23. We see it with Joseph and the other sons of Jacob in Genesis 37-43. In fact, Judah and his brothers sold Joseph into slavery, trying to thwart the plan of God that would cause them to bow before their younger brother. Doing so, however, eventually brought about the very results God had intended. In Judah's own family, his wicked older sons died and his younger sons carried on the family heritage. God gave Tamar twins and the line of Judah continued because of her. Finally David, the youngest of all of Jesse's sons, the one forgotten in the field tending the sheep, is the one who is chosen to be king. God's will works out in pointed confirmation of the principle that the elder serves the younger.

Torah Codes in Genesis 38

There's more. I found an article called "Codes in the Torah" when I was in Russia attending a meeting of an association of religious professionals from the Soviet Union. This was in 1987, but I was flabbergasted with this little discovery. We find the story of Judah and Tamar in Genesis 38. It is there we learn the history of Pharez and Zarah, and therefore the entire tribe of Judah. When we examine Genesis 38 (and remember that the Hebrew language reads from right to left) we find the names of David's genealogy coded there centuries before the king was born. At an interim of 49 letters, we first get the name BOAZ. We might consider this just an interesting coincidence, but if we count again in 49-letter intervals, we find the name RUTH.

Both names are encrypted in Genesis 38 long before the events of Joshua, Judges, Ruth or 1 Samuel took place. It doesn't stop there, though. Also at 49-letter intervals, we can find the name of OBED, and again at 49-letter intervals we find YISSHAI (Jesse). Finally, at 49-letter intervals again we can find the name DAVID. All together we have the names of Boaz, Ruth, Obed, Jesse, and David, each with an interval of 49-letters. They are in chronological order, and all this was all penned before any of them were born, in the very chapter of the Bible that relates the story behind the birth of their ancestor Pharez. This has staggering implications when we think it through.

Genesis 38

1 וַיְהִי בָּעֵת הַהִוא וַיֵּרֶד יְהוּדָה מֵאֵת אֶחָיו וַיֵּט עַד אִישׁ עֲדֻלָּמִי וּשְׁמוֹ חִירָה:
2 וַיַּרְא שָׁם יְהוּדָה בַּת אִישׁ כְּנַעֲנִי וּשְׁמוֹ שׁוּעַ וַיִּקָּחֶהָ וַיָּבֹא אֵלֶיהָ:
3 וַתַּהַר וַתֵּלֶד בֵּן וַיִּקְרָא אֶת שְׁמוֹ עֵר:
4 וַתַּהַר עוֹד וַתֵּלֶד בֵּן וַתִּקְרָא אֶת שְׁמוֹ אוֹנָן:
5 וַתֹּסֶף עוֹד וַתֵּלֶד בֵּן וַתִּקְרָא אֶת שְׁמוֹ שֵׁלָה וְהָיָה בִכְזִיב בְּלִדְתָּהּ אֹתוֹ:
6 וַיִּקַּח יְהוּדָה אִשָּׁה לְעֵר בְּכוֹרוֹ וּשְׁמָהּ תָּמָר:
7 וַיְהִי עֵר בְּכוֹר יְהוּדָה רַע בְּעֵינֵי יְהוָה וַיְמִתֵהוּ יְהוָה: — **בעז** Boaz
8 וַיֹּאמֶר יְהוּדָה לְאוֹנָן בֹּא אֶל אֵשֶׁת אָחִיךָ וְיַבֵּם אֹתָהּ וְהָקֵם זֶרַע לְאָחִיךָ:
9 וַיֵּדַע אוֹנָן כִּי לֹּא לוֹ יִהְיֶה הַזָּרַע וְהָיָה אִם בָּא אֶל אֵשֶׁת אָחִיו וְשִׁחֵת אַרְצָה לְבִלְתִּי נְתָן זֶרַע לְאָחִיו:
10 וַיֵּרַע בְּעֵינֵי יְהוָה אֲשֶׁר עָשָׂה וַיָּמֶת גַּם אֹתוֹ:
11 וַיֹּאמֶר יְהוּדָה לְתָמָר כַּלָּתוֹ שְׁבִי אַלְמָנָה בֵית אָבִיךְ עַד יִגְדַּל שֵׁלָה בְנִי כִּי אָמַר פֶּן יָמוּת גַּם הוּא כְּאֶחָיו וַתֵּלֶךְ תָּמָר וַתֵּשֶׁב בֵּית אָבִיהָ:
12 וַיִּרְבּוּ הַיָּמִים וַתָּמָת בַּת שׁוּעַ אֵשֶׁת יְהוּדָה וַיִּנָּחֶם יְהוּדָה וַיַּעַל עַל גֹּזְזֵי צֹאנוֹ הוּא וְחִירָה רֵעֵהוּ הָעֲדֻלָּמִי תִּמְנָתָה: — **רות** Ruth
13 וַיֻּגַּד לְתָמָר לֵאמֹר הִנֵּה חָמִיךְ עֹלֶה תִמְנָתָה לָגֹז צֹאנוֹ:
14 וַתָּסַר בִּגְדֵי אַלְמְנוּתָהּ מֵעָלֶיהָ וַתְּכַס בַּצָּעִיף וַתִּתְעַלָּף וַתֵּשֶׁב בְּפֶתַח עֵינַיִם אֲשֶׁר עַל דֶּרֶךְ תִּמְנָתָה כִּי רָאֲתָה כִּי גָדַל שֵׁלָה וְהִוא לֹא נִתְּנָה לוֹ לְאִשָּׁה:
15 וַיִּרְאֶהָ יְהוּדָה וַיַּחְשְׁבֶהָ לְזוֹנָה כִּי כִסְּתָה פָּנֶיהָ:
16 וַיֵּט אֵלֶיהָ אֶל הַדֶּרֶךְ וַיֹּאמֶר הָבָה נָּא אָבוֹא אֵלַיִךְ כִּי לֹא יָדַע כִּי כַלָּתוֹ הִוא וַתֹּאמֶר מַה תִּתֶּן לִי כִּי תָבוֹא אֵלָי: — **עבד** Obed
17 וַיֹּאמֶר אָנֹכִי אֲשַׁלַּח גְּדִי עִזִּים מִן הַצֹּאן וַתֹּאמֶר אִם תִּתֵּן עֵרָבוֹן עַד שָׁלְחֶךָ:
18 וַיֹּאמֶר מָה הָעֵרָבוֹן אֲשֶׁר אֶתֶּן לָךְ וַתֹּאמֶר חֹתָמְךָ וּפְתִילֶךָ וּמַטְּךָ אֲשֶׁר בְּיָדֶךָ וַיִּתֶּן לָהּ וַיָּבֹא אֵלֶיהָ וַתַּהַר לוֹ:
19 וַתָּקָם וַתֵּלֶךְ וַתָּסַר צְעִיפָהּ מֵעָלֶיהָ וַתִּלְבַּשׁ בִּגְדֵי אַלְמְנוּתָהּ:
20 וַיִּשְׁלַח יְהוּדָה אֶת גְּדִי הָעִזִּים בְּיַד רֵעֵהוּ הָעֲדֻלָּמִי לָקַחַת הָעֵרָבוֹן מִיַּד הָאִשָּׁה וְלֹא מְצָאָהּ:
21 וַיִּשְׁאַל אֶת אַנְשֵׁי מְקֹמָהּ לֵאמֹר אַיֵּה הַקְּדֵשָׁה הִוא בָעֵינַיִם עַל הַדָּרֶךְ וַיֹּאמְרוּ לֹא הָיְתָה בָזֶה קְדֵשָׁה:
22 וַיָּשָׁב אֶל יְהוּדָה וַיֹּאמֶר לֹא מְצָאתִיהָ וְגַם אַנְשֵׁי הַמָּקוֹם אָמְרוּ לֹא הָיְתָה בָזֶה קְדֵשָׁה:
23 וַיֹּאמֶר יְהוּדָה תִּקַּח לָהּ פֶּן נִהְיֶה לָבוּז הִנֵּה שָׁלַחְתִּי הַגְּדִי הַזֶּה וְאַתָּה לֹא מְצָאתָהּ:
24 וַיְהִי כְּמִשְׁלֹשׁ חֳדָשִׁים וַיֻּגַּד לִיהוּדָה לֵאמֹר זָנְתָה תָּמָר כַּלָּתֶךָ וְגַם הִנֵּה הָרָה לִזְנוּנִים וַיֹּאמֶר יְהוּדָה הוֹצִיאוּהָ וְתִשָּׂרֵף: — **ישי** Yishay (Jesse)
25 הִוא מוּצֵאת וְהִיא שָׁלְחָה אֶל חָמִיהָ לֵאמֹר לְאִישׁ אֲשֶׁר אֵלֶּה לּוֹ אָנֹכִי הָרָה וַתֹּאמֶר הַכֶּר נָא לְמִי הַחֹתֶמֶת וְהַפְּתִילִים וְהַמַּטֶּה הָאֵלֶּה:
26 וַיַּכֵּר יְהוּדָה וַיֹּאמֶר צָדְקָה מִמֶּנִּי כִּי עַל כֵּן לֹא נְתַתִּיהָ לְשֵׁלָה בְנִי וְלֹא יָסַף עוֹד לְדַעְתָּהּ:
27 וַיְהִי בְּעֵת לִדְתָּהּ וְהִנֵּה תְאוֹמִים בְּבִטְנָהּ:
28 וַיְהִי בְלִדְתָּהּ וַיִּתֶּן יָד וַתִּקַּח הַמְיַלֶּדֶת וַתִּקְשֹׁר עַל יָדוֹ שָׁנִי לֵאמֹר זֶה יָצָא רִאשֹׁנָה:
29 וַיְהִי כְּמֵשִׁיב יָדוֹ וְהִנֵּה יָצָא אָחִיו וַתֹּאמֶר מַה פָּרַצְתָּ עָלֶיךָ פָּרֶץ וַיִּקְרָא שְׁמוֹ פָּרֶץ: — **דוד** David
30 וְאַחַר יָצָא אָחִיו אֲשֶׁר עַל יָדוֹ הַשָּׁנִי וַיִּקְרָא שְׁמוֹ זָרַח:

בעז	Boaz
רות	Ruth
עבד	Obed
ישי	Jesse
דוד	David

*All in 49-letter intervals: &
All in <u>chronological</u> order!*

Love's Reward

89

Every word, every place name, every jot and tittle in the Bible is precious. As we find these things hidden away for centuries before King David was born, we begin to recognize just how truly awesome the Bible is. Not only was David purposed in God's heart before his grandfather was born, but the Son of David, the King of Kings, was ordained as our Kinsman Redeemer from the foundation of the earth.[11] That should astound us all.

---

[11] 1 Peter 1:20; Revelation 13:8

Chapter 7
Selah Moments

This story of Ruth and Boaz and Naomi really happened. These were real people who lived this narrative. However, the symbolic imagery that the Book of Ruth provides is astonishing. Allusions abound in the story of Boaz, Naomi and Ruth to the greater purposes of God in Christ, Israel, and the Church. We've touched on these things, but I want to summarize them in full here.

Boaz is clearly the kinsman-redeemer in this story, the type of Christ. He's in the role of the *go'el*, just as Jesus Christ is our Kinsman-Redeemer. This does not mean that he was an Old Testament appearance of Christ, of course, but rather that his role gives us perspective about our own Kinsman-Redeemer. Boaz represents the role of Jesus Christ here.

Boaz was a real man who lived during the time of the judges. His gracious love of Ruth, however, reminds us of the gracious love that Christ has for the Church. We were Gentiles, separated from God, but through grace, Christ brought us in and loved us. It seems unusual that Boaz would readily take a Moabitess as a wife, but when we realize that his own mother was Rahab the harlot, we see how Boaz might understand God's grace better than most.

Israel is not left out of this. Naomi is a blessing to Ruth, for without Naomi, Ruth would never have found her husband, just as we would never have found our Savior without Israel. The marriage of Boaz to Ruth blessed Naomi, just as the Church is a blessing to Israel.

The Church versus Israel

There are things we should appreciate about the distinction between the roles of Naomi and Ruth. They are both loved. They are both provided for. The Kinsman-Redeemer rescues them both. Yet, they have different roles, and different purposes to fulfill. Consider these facts:

- Naomi had to be exiled from her land in order to bring Ruth home into the family.
- Grace accomplished what the Law could not.
- Ruth does not replace Naomi. The events of the story benefit them both.
- It is Naomi who tells Ruth how to approach Boaz.
- Yet, Naomi meets Boaz because of Ruth.
- Boaz loves Ruth from the beginning, but he awaits her move.
- Boaz, not Ruth, confronts the "nearer kinsman."

In Chapter 1, Ruth has no clue that Boaz exists.

In Chapter 2, Ruth sees herself as a lowly servant, gleaning in fields to feed her mother-in-law. She only knows Boaz as a wealthy, mighty man who shows her kindness.

In Chapter 3, Ruth obeys Naomi's instructions and places herself at the feet of Boaz. Then, she believes his promises.

In Chapter 4, Boaz claims and purchases Ruth as his wife. She is no longer a poor servant; everything that belongs to Boaz now belongs to her.

Too many of God's people are willing to remain forever trapped in Chapter 2, picking up the leftovers when God has so much more for them. God is willing to bless them with all spiritual blessings in Christ Jesus, but rather than focusing on the Giver, they are focusing on the scraps they pick from the ground. It would make all the difference if they would only surrender to the Lord and look to the Giver rather than to the gifts.

Ruth versus Esther

Considering the times in which it was written, the Bible gives a remarkable amount of honor to faithful women in its history. When we compare Ruth and Esther, we find an interesting parallel.

Ruth was a Gentile woman living among Jews. Esther was a Jewish woman living among Gentiles. Ruth married a Jew (Boaz) in a royal line who would rule an empire. Esther married a Gentile (Ahasuerus) in a royal line that already ruled an empire. Ruth emphasizes the providence of God. Esther emphasizes the sovereignty of God.

In both stories, courageous, faithful women trusted God and obeyed those who spoke wisdom into their lives. In both stories, these women were willing to sacrifice themselves for others. And both stories demonstrate that God is working undercover behind the scenes to bring about His will and the salvation of His people.

The Title Deed of Planet Earth

Remember that there were four requirements of the *go'el*: he had to be a kinsman, he had to be willing, he had to be able, and he had to assume all the obligations involved. The role of Boaz as kinsman-redeemer describes our own Savior, the one who rescues us and pulls us from the dirt. There is more here than just a fulfillment of the Laws of Redemption and Levirate Marriage in ancient Israel, however. We can take the lessons learned here and look ahead to the greatest real estate redemption of all time – the one we find in Revelation 5.

> *And I saw in the right hand of him that sat on the throne a book written within and on the backside, sealed with seven seals. And I saw a strong angel proclaiming with a loud voice, Who is worthy to open the book, and to loose the seals thereof? And no man in heaven, nor in earth, neither under the earth, was able to open*

*the book, neither to look thereon. And I
wept much, because no man was found
worthy to open and to read the book,
neither to look thereon.*

Revelation 5:1-4

The scroll sounds like a title scroll, written both on the inside and the outside. Notice that it had to be a man, a kinsman of Adam, to break the seals of the scroll. Yet, no man was found who was worthy to open the scroll. There was none found who had the means of redeeming the entire earth. We don't really understand that, but John did because he sobs convulsively. This is a mystery thriller of the first kind. This scroll also potentially lists the inventory of heaven, earth, and beneath the earth. Only a kinsman of Adam had the right to open the scroll, but no kinsman of Adam was found who had the power to purchase back the land. Therefore John wept convulsively, until one of the 24 elders spoke to him:

*And one of the elders saith unto me, Weep
not: behold, the Lion of the tribe of Juda,
the Root of David, hath prevailed to
open the book, and to loose the seven seals
thereof. And I behold, and, lo, in the midst
of the throne and of the four beasts, and
in the midst of the elders, stood a Lamb as
it had been slain, having seven horns and
seven eyes, which are the seven Spirits of
God sent forth into all the earth.*

Revelation 5:5-6

These are all Jewish titles. The Lamb is not referred to as the "Lion of the tribe of Judah" or as the "Root of David" in the letters to the Seven Churches. Jesus took the role of a sacrificial Lamb at His First Coming. With that act He made the payment for all of us – He bought back that which was lost. He alone is both a kinsman of Adam and worthy to open the scrolls. At His Second Coming, He will behave like a lion. He will come as a conqueror, as the Lion of Judah returning to take the throne of His father David.

> *And he came and took the book out of the right hand of him that sat upon the throne. And when he had taken the book, the four beasts and four and twenty elders fell down before the Lamb, having every one of them harps, and golden vials full of odours, which are the prayers of saints.*
>
> Revelation 5:7-8

The Lamb comes and takes the scroll, and as He does, everybody falls down to worship Him. Not only are those present involved, but our own prayers have been collected in vials and are added to the beautiful aroma of the worship before the Throne.

The word "beasts" here is a poor translation, by the way. These are the cherubim, the four "living creatures" of Ezekiel 1. John also calls them "living ones" using the Greek word ζῷον - *zōon*. These four living beings stand before God's throne full of love for the Creator.

> *And they sung a new song, saying,*
> *Thou art worthy to take the book,*
> *and to open the seals thereof: for thou*
> *wast slain, and hast redeemed us to God*
> *by thy blood out of every kindred, and*
> *tongue, and people, and nation; And hast*
> *made us unto our God kings and priests:*
> *and we shall reign on the earth.*
>
> Revelation 5:9-10

He has redeemed us by His blood. He has redeemed us, and He has given us everything, just as Ruth gained all that Boaz had when he redeemed her and she became his. Revelation 1:5-6 identifies those that are kings and priests: they are us. They are those who are washed from their sins in His blood.

> *And I beheld, and I heard the voice of*
> *many angels round about the throne*
> *and the beasts and the elders: and the*
> *number of them was ten thousand times*
> *ten thousand, and thousands of thousands;*
> *Saying with a loud voice, Worthy is the*
> *Lamb that was slain to receive power,*
> *and riches, and wisdom, and strength,*
> *and honour, and glory, and blessing.*
> *And every creature which is in heaven,*
> *and on the earth, and under the earth,*

*and such as are in the sea, and all that
are in them, heard I saying, Blessing,
and honour, and glory, and power,
be unto him that sitteth upon the throne,
and unto the Lamb for ever and ever.
And the four beasts said, Amen. And the
four and twenty elders fell down and
worshipped him that liveth for ever
and ever.*

Revelation 5:11-14

Here Jesus is worshiped for who He really is. He is no longer lying in a manger in Bethlehem, nor hanging on a cross as the punishment for our sins, nor dead in the tomb. He is the risen Son of Almighty God. He takes the center position of worship because of who He is and for what He has done and what He is still doing. Here in Revelation, He also takes on the role as Avenger of Blood. He will shortly come to punish the cruel wickedness committed by those who do not fear Him.

Our redemption is sealed. He's our Kinsman-Redeemer. However, Christ, like Boaz, waits for us. He does not move on our behalf until we claim Him as our Kinsman-Redeemer. Not one of us should close this day without making that claim. We have the right. He is our Kinsman, a Son of Adam, and He is the only one able to pay the debt against us. He loves us dearly, and He is just waiting for us to delight Him by making our move and lying down at His feet.

If you have never gone to Him and sought Him, don't let the day close without doing so. In your own way go before Him and claim Him as your Kinsman-Redeemer. Christ died on a cross for you, and even today He stands at the door of your heart saying, as in Revelation 3:20:

Behold, I stand at the door, and knock: if any man hear my voice, and open the door, I will come in to him, and will sup with him, and he with me.

That's His commitment. He won't crash your door down. It's your move. Just as Boaz went to council on behalf of Ruth, Jesus goes on our behalf. He speaks up for us and He takes care of all the confusing details. He's just waiting for us to ask.

Grace accomplished what the Law could not. Ruth did not replace Naomi, but the two blessed one another and led each other to their mutual redemption. Ruth learned the ways of Boaz through Naomi, but Naomi met Boaz through Ruth.

This is why the Book of Ruth is one of the most fruitful stories in Scripture. This is why it ranks among my very favorite books of the Bible. We cannot read through it without learning something new. I have studied through this book at least 100 times, and yet each time I glean something I hadn't seen before. It's unfathomable, and I do not believe I'll find the end of it.

The Romance of Redemption

> *Wherefore he is able also to save them to the uttermost that come unto God by him, seeing he ever liveth to make intercession for them.*
>
> Hebrews 2:25

You and I are beneficiaries of a love story that was written in blood on a wooden cross erected in Judea some 2,000 years ago. Much more is at stake than just you and me and our salvation. The creation itself, a new heaven and a new earth are at risk here. "Because of a wooden cross in Judea."

I'm not a Republican or a Democrat. I'm a monarchist. My candidate is the King of the Jews. Yes, He is a racial king. Let's not forget that Jesus is Jewish, and he is King of the Jews – and from Jerusalem, King of the entire world. He is a prophet before Moses, a priest after Melchizedek, a champion like Joshua, an offering in the place of Isaac, a King from the line of David, a wise counselor above Solomon. He was beloved, rejected, and then exalted, in a manner that goes far beyond the suffering and glorification of Joseph. He was the voice of the burning bush. He's the Captain of the LORD's host. He was the conqueror of Jericho. He's endearingly strong, entirely sincere, eternally steadfast, immortally graceful, imperially powerful, and impartially merciful.

Colossians 2:9 tells us that in Him dwells the fullness of the Godhead bodily. Jesus is very God of very God. He's our High Priest, our personal prophet, our reigning King.

Jesus is not just a concept or a tradition. He's a living person who is about to return to take His throne.

He was crucified on a cross of wood, yet He made the hill on which it stood. What held Him to that cross were not the nails, but His love for you and me. It wasn't only His own love, but the love of the Father who chose to endure His Son being tortured to death.

> *Let's bow our hearts. Father, we stagger as we try to apprehend the extremes You've gone to on our behalf; the giving of Your Son that we might live. We stagger as we try to grasp what You've done for us. Words fail. We just thank you, Father, for who You are. We thank You that we serve a God who is merciful, who is gracious, who has done everything for us. Father, we thank You for Your Word, and we thank You for Your Spirit to reveal that Word to us. Help us, Father, to appropriate these things into our lives, that we each might be more effective stewards of the opportunities You bring across our path, that we each might be more effective for You and more pleasing in Your sight as we commit, with no reservations whatsoever, ourselves, into Your hands. In the name of Yeshua, our Kinsman-Redeemer indeed. Amen.*

Bibliography

Bull, Geoffrey T., *Love Song in Harvest*, Christian Literature Crusade, Fort Washington PA, 19034, 1972.

Bullinger, E.W., *The Companion Bible*, Zondervan Bible Publishers, Grand Rapids, MI, 1958.

Campbell, Edward F. Jr., *Ruth*, Doubleday & Co., Garden City NY, 1975.

DeHaan, M.R., *The Romance of Redemption*, Zondervan Publishing House, Grand Rapids MI, 1958.

Fruchtenbaum, Arnold G.: *Ariel's Bible Commentary: The Books of Judges and Ruth*. 1st ed. San Antonio, Tex. : Ariel Ministries, 2006.

Henry, Matthew and Thomas Scott, *Commentary on the Holy Bible*, Thomas Nelson Publishing Company, NY, 1979.

Heslop, W.G., *Rubies from Ruth*, Zondervan Publishing House, 1944.

Hession, Roy, *Our Nearest Kinsman*, Christian Literature Crusade, Fort Washington PA, 19034, 1976.

Jamieson, Rev. Robert, Rev. A.R. Fausset and Rev. David Brown, *A Commentary Critical, Experimental, and Practical on the Old and New Testaments*, vol. V, William B. Eerdman's Publishing Company, Grand Rapids, MI, 1948.

McGee, J. Vernon, *Ruth, Thru the Bible Books*, Box 100, Pasadena CA, 91109, 1976.

Pfeiffer, Charles F.: T*he Wycliffe Bible Commentary: Old Testament*, Chicago, Moody Press, 1962.

Scofield, C.I., *The New Scofield Study Bible*, (KJV) Oxford University Press, New York, 1967.

Spence, H.D.M. and Joseph S. Exell (editors), *The Pulpit Commentary*, vol. 15 - Matthew, William B. Eerdmans Publishing Company, Grand Rapids, MI, 1961.

Walvoord, John F., and Zuck, Roy B., *The Bible Knowledge Commentary*, (Wheaton, Illinois: Scripture Press Publications, Inc.) 1983, 1985. (Also available on Logos 2.0, Level 4.)

About the Author

Chuck Missler
*President/Founder,
Koinonia House*

Chuck Missler was raised in Southern California.

Chuck demonstrated an aptitude for technical interests as a youth. He became a ham radio operator at age nine and started piloting airplanes as a teenager. While still in high school, Chuck built a digital computer in the family garage.

His plans to pursue a doctorate in electrical engineering at Stanford University were interrupted when he received a Congressional appointment to the United States Naval Academy at Annapolis. Graduating with honors, Chuck took his commission in the Air Force. After completing flight training, he met and married Nancy (who later founded The King's High Way ministry). Chuck joined the Missile Program and eventually became Branch Chief of the Department of Guided Missiles.

Chuck made the transition from the military to the private sector when he became a systems engineer with TRW, a large aerospace firm. He then went on to serve as a senior analyst with a non-profit think tank where he conducted projects for the intelligence community and the Department of Defense. During that time, Chuck earned a master's degree in engineering at UCLA, supplementing previous graduate work in applied mathematics, advanced statistics and information sciences.

Recruited into senior management at the Ford Motor Company in Dearborn, Michigan, Chuck established the first international computer network in 1966. He left Ford to start his own company, a computer network firm that was subsequently acquired by Automatic Data Processing (listed on the New York Stock Exchange) to become its Network Services Division.

As Chuck notes, his day of reckoning came in the early '90s when — as the result of a merger — he found himself the chairman and a major shareholder of a small, publicly owned development company known as Phoenix Group International. The firm established an $8 billion joint venture with the Soviet Union to supply personal computers to their 143,000 schools. Due to several unforeseen circumstances, the venture failed. The Misslers lost everything, including their home, automobiles and insurance.

It was during this difficult time that Chuck turned to God and the Bible. As a child he developed an intense interest in the Bible; studying it became a favorite pastime. In the 1970s, while still in the corporate world, Chuck began leading weekly Bible studies at the 30,000 member Calvary Chapel Costa Mesa, in California. He and Nancy established Koinonia House in 1973, an organization devoted to encouraging people to study the Bible.

Chuck had enjoyed a longtime, personal relationship with Hal Lindsey, who upon hearing of Chuck's professional misfortune, convinced him that he could easily succeed as an independent author and speaker. Over the years, Chuck had developed a loyal following. (Through Doug Wetmore, head of the tape ministry of Firefighters for Christ, Chuck learned that over 7 million copies of his taped Bible studies were scattered throughout the world.) Koinonia House then became Chuck's full-time profession.

Other Resources

Learn the Bible

Are you ready for a detailed yet thoroughly enjoyable study of the most profound book ever written?

Using sound scientific facts, historical analysis, and Biblical narrative, acclaimed teacher Dr. Chuck Missler weaves together a rich tapestry of information—providing an accurate understanding of Scripture's relation to itself, to us and to the world at large.

Examine the heroic tales of Exodus, the lasting wisdom of Proverbs, or even the enigmatic imagery of Revelation with the simple, Scripturally sound insights and fresh perspectives found in *Learn the Bible in 24 Hours*. Whether you want to explore some of the less-discussed nuances of Scripture or you need a comprehensive refresher course on the Bible's themes and stories, *Learn the Bible in 24 Hours* is a great guide.

Available from https://Resources.khouse.org

Other Resources

Hidden Treasures

For the novice as well as the sophisticate, this book is full of surprises. It includes subtle discoveries lying just "beneath" the text – hidden messages, encryptions, deliberate misspellings and other amendments to the text – that present implications beyond the immediate context, demonstrating a skillful design that has its origin from outside our space and time. Drawing upon over forty years of collecting, Chuck highlights in this book many of the precious nuggets that have become characteristic of his popular Bible studies around the world.

It is guaranteed to stimulate, provoke, and, hopefully, to disturb. It will confound the skeptic and encourage the believer. It is a "must read" for every thinking seeker of truth and serious inquirer of reality.

Available from https://Resources.khouse.org